THE HISTORY OF ROYAL WINDSOR RACECOURSE

JIM BEAVIS

This edition first published in Great Britain in 2016 by Jim Beavis c/o Royal Windsor Racecourse, Maidenhead Road, Windsor, Berkshire SL4 5JJ. Email: office@windsor-racecourse.co.uk and jimbeavis@hotmail.com

ISBN 978-0-9543322-5-9

A catalogue record for this book is available from the British Library
Printed and bound by Weatherbys, Sanders Road, Wellingborough, Northants NN8 4BX

CONTENTS

PROLOGUE

1 July 1944. A large crowd was enjoying a pleasant summer's day at Windsor races. Thirteen runners had finished walking round the leafy paddock and were about to go down to the start for the 3.30 when a strange low growl became increasingly audible. People looked around to try to work out where it was coming from. An announcement over the public address warned that a flying bomb was approaching and that people should take cover. Some ran towards the stands, others dived to the ground. The sound of the bomb's engine grew louder, and then stopped. In the pregnant silence everyone waited for it to drop out of the sky, and braced themselves for the inevitable explosion.

CHAPTER 1
ROYAL WINDSOR

It has been "Royal" Windsor from the very beginning of racing on Rays Meadow, the island formed by the river Thames to the north and the Mill Stream to the south, in 1866. While members of the royal family are seen here from time to time – the late Queen Mother was especially partial to popping down from the Castle – the connection between royalty, racing and Windsor goes back hundreds of years. But there is no stuffiness about proceedings here. Win or lose, the smart yet relaxed ambience of a summer Monday evening is the ideal tonic after the first day of the working week. The trees, the impeccably neat lawns and the abundance of places to eat, drink and sit makes it a destination thousands love to return to.

One of its unique virtues is the ability to arrive on its doorstep by ferry, whether you have made the journey by the slow train from Waterloo to the Riverside station, or the swifter Paddington-change-at-Slough-Windsor & Eton Central route.

Until the 1960s rail travellers would head for where taxis now queue beside the Castle. Then there used to be buses waiting to take them most of the way to the course, leaving them a half mile walk from a coach park. But now a short walk from either station brings you to the riverside kiosk of French Brothers. All year round their boats take tourists on a variety of cruises to enjoy the pleasant Berkshire scenery. The voyage to the racecourse only takes about ten minutes.

Few passengers take much notice of the little opening on the left almost immediately after passing under the second bridge. That is the Mill Stream, which runs parallel with the Thames. It carries on westward along the edge of the secluded Clewer village, which used to house the stables for the racecourse and the Royal Windsor Horse Show. It's this stream that makes the racecourse an island. The driveway up to the stands and the members' car park has a bridge crossing over it. The stream meanders on towards the intersection of the racetrack's figure of eight and then sticks close to the southern edge of the loop, passing the marina before rejoining the Thames immediately beyond the furthest end of the loop.

Resuming our boat trip on the Thames, immediately after the Mill Stream is White Lilies Island, which the singer Natalie Imbruglia, its most famous resident, used for the title of her second album. After that the Clewer Mill House should be visible, where the actor Michael Caine and Led Zeppelin guitarist Jimmy Page used to live. For almost a century its grounds could be crossed by pedestrians en route to the racecourse on payment of a toll. Mrs Mosscockle, who lived there in the 1920s, was a local character who when being chauffeured round in her Daimler would wave at people as though she was royalty. Her horses and dogs are thought to be buried somewhere in the grounds of what was in the past a large estate.

At Clewer Point the Thames turns abruptly right. A jetty appears straight ahead, the boat slows down, and we've arrived – already. Racegoers disembark and face a short walk past the back of the weighing room to the main entrance. A second landing stage fifty yards further on is for private parties arriving at the track.

The river was a means of transport from the early days of the race meeting. Boats have also carried passengers from Staines and Maidenhead. Benign though it looks, the river is dangerous. A day-tripper from London, George Pearson, drowned when bathing by the racecourse in 1886. A posse of Etonians swimming nearby went to his aid, but failed to rescue him in time.

Here a word should be said about Arthur Jacobs, who was born in 1863 and lived in Windsor and Eton most of his life. He was a keen swimmer and as an eight-year-old boy helped bring two little girls to safety who were struggling in the Thames. Another time he assisted with the rescue of two boys in the water close to the racecourse. Altogether he is believed to have helped over sixty people at risk of drowning and he received several awards. More about his exploits, and indeed everything to do with the history of the town of Windsor can be found on the excellent theroyalwindsorforum.yuku.com website. Jacobs started a ferryboat business and built the Thames Hotel near the Promenade, which is now Brown's restaurant. In the 1960s French Brothers took over.

Nowadays there is a happy relationship between them, the racecourse, the police and the local authority. The ferries help reduce road traffic and are environmentally friendly. From French Brothers' point of view, Monday evening race meetings are ideal, as it is a quiet day of the week otherwise. They run as many boats to the racecourse as they think necessary, using last year's passenger statistics as a guide, and extend their timetables to accommodate the late finishes in midsummer.

Those who go back to Paddington should look out for Station Jim on platform 5 at Slough. Jim, who is stuffed, used to be a railway collection dog. These were dogs that lived at major stations with wooden collecting boxes strapped to their backs. Station Jim accepted donations (with a bark) to the Great Western Railway widows and orphans charity. He worked for only two years at Slough before he died in 1896, but was so popular that money was raised to have him stuffed and put in a display case. He was regarded as a very clever dog, which is true judging by some of his comments on his Twitter account.

***

Windsor Castle dates from the reign of William the Conqueror (1066-87) and has been used as a home for English monarchs for almost 900 years. Windsor itself is believed to have been the site of a small settlement since the 7th century, where it's thought that members of the ruling Anglo-Saxon classes had reason to visit well before the Castle was built. Hunting was a very popular royal sport in medieval times, and the closeness of good hunting country (Windsor Forest, now the Great Park) no doubt added to the attraction of the area.

Racing took place there under various horse-loving monarchs. Edward III sold some of his stallions in the 1360s to help pay for the substantial rebuilding of the Castle. Henry VIII, a sportsman with competitive instincts to match those of his private life and his diplomatic career, kept a racing stable and a stud within its grounds. These were probably Arabians, as this was well before the development of the thoroughbred. He splashed out on prize money and travelling allowances for visiting racehorses – or rather, his loyal subjects did, as this was all funded by taxes.

Henry retained a gentleman rider called Thomas Ogle. Professional jockeys were unheard of at this time. His trainer Powle was paid £20 a year but he considered this was not enough, judging by the extra expenses he claimed, such as 7s 2d in 1532 for bathing one of the horses. In view of Henry's ruthless manner of disposing of wives, churchmen or indeed anybody else who crossed him, Powle was playing with fire.

Queen Elizabeth I maintained the family interest in racing, adding stables at Greenwich, Waltham, St Albans, Oaklands, Eton, Richmond, Hampton Court and Charing Cross. In her tours across the country to visit her archbishops the clergy found more favour if they laid on some races for her amusement.

After the puritanical Cromwell years when Christmas celebrations and sport were banned, the nation breathed a collective sigh of relief when the fun-loving Charles II took the throne in 1660. Before long his ministers were muttering about him taking too much of an interest in racing by holding court frequently in Newmarket, whose emergence as the headquarters of British racing is due to him. Charles himself rode a couple of winners there and founded the Newmarket Town Plate in 1665, which is still an important annual event in the town.

London to Newmarket or vice versa could entail a detour to Windsor, where Datchet Ferry (also sometimes referred to as Dorsett) to the north east of the Castle had become the location for the races. Gambling was, inevitably, part of the fun, and 500 guineas was bet on one race in 1682. There is a story that when Charles was at Windsor Nell Gwyn used to stay at the Old Bridge House across the river from Datchet, because the Queen refused to have Nell living in the same county. Sadly there is no evidence to support this tale.

The meeting on 24 August 1684 is the subject of a much-reproduced etching made by Francis Barlow in 1687. Charles and the Duke of York can be seen watching from their bijou private stand, a temporary wooden structure. Though it purports to be "the last Horse Race run before Charles II of Blessed Memory", he undoubtedly saw others while he was in Newmarket that October; Barlow must mean it was the last he saw at Windsor. Surrounding the picture are his fawning verses:-

> To future times may these illustrious Sports
> Be only the divertisement of Courts,
> Since the best Man, best Judge, and best of Kings,
> Whose President, the best example brings,
> When ere his Godlike mind unbent from care,
> To all his pleasures this he would prefer ....

There is more in the same vein. A more impudent poet wrote the following after Charles's death. It is probably about a different course, but it is just as applicable to Datchet.

> Next, for the glory of the place,
> Here has been rode many a race:
> King Charles the Second I saw here,
> But I've forgotten in what year:

After a few years of royal indifference Queen Anne was the next race-loving monarch. She reigned from 1702 to 1714, racing her own horses and enjoying race meetings when not otherwise engaged in conceiving eighteen children, only one of whom survived beyond the age of eleven. The gloriously named Narcissus Luttrell, a Member of

Parliament and assiduous gossip-gatherer, wrote in 1705 that Anne and her husband, Prince George of Denmark "seem mightily given to racing. The Queen has appointed a horse race to be at Datchet after her return from Winchester to Windsor." In 1709 he wrote about "a great horse race at Datchet. Colonel Moreton won the Queen's Plate and the Earl of Bridgewater that of the town of Windsor." Interestingly it was run on 24 August, the same day as the 1684 meeting pictured by Barlow.

In 1711 Anne was travelling across an expanse of open heathland at East Cote, a few miles west of Windsor, and thought it would make a good racecourse. The first event, with a £100 prize endowed by Her Majesty took place that August. Thus East Cote, or rather Ascot races were born.

By the time she died Parliament had already taken steps to ensure that the throne did not pass to a Catholic. Using circuitous logic a Protestant cousin who ruled the German city-state of Hanover had been lined up as a suitable successor. Neither he nor his son (George I and II) were interested in racing and any that took place at Windsor itself was of parochial interest only. That did not stop Ascot quickly became the centre of racing in Berkshire; the aristocracy were keen enough for the monarchs' lack of interest not to matter. It was not until 1768 was the Royal prefix was applied.

A race meeting was held at Englefield Green in 1729 and in 1734 one nominally at Egham was held on the Runnymede. "Mede" means meadow, but the first part of the name is nothing to do with "running". It is believed to come from the Anglo-Saxon "runieg" meaning a regular meeting – hence it was a logical place for the Magna Carta to be agreed. It was a coincidence that meetings of an equine nature were held there for over a hundred years. The Egham meeting folded in 1740 when a new law imposed a number of restrictions on racing (because of its "encouragement of idleness" and "impoverishment of many of the meaner sort of the subjects of the kingdom"). Another of its measures compelled most race meetings to offer minimum prize money. Quite a few other courses fell by the wayside as a result of that. Even Ascot could not afford to race for a few years.

Windsor was able to race lawfully by offering £50 prizes in 1744, 1745, 1747 and 1766. The local corporation put up £50 in 1769. Racing was over long distances (three or four miles), with few runners, so each race consisted of two or more heats which were often run at a very steady pace for all but the last half mile or so. Generally the first horse to win two heats took the spoils.

There was no town or village to speak of by the Ascot racecourse and as the meeting there grew in prestige, the nearby towns of Windsor, Egham and Sunninghill were where racegoers stayed, walking to Ascot each day if they could not afford a horse or carriage. Those towns also hosted Ordinaries – set-price public dinners – as well as theatre, gambling dens, cock-fighting and all the other entertainments that might be appreciated by a large contingent of mostly-male visitors with money in their pockets. Every hotel in the area was full in Ascot week, and any spare beds for miles around could be let at a premium.

The people of Windsor and other towns and villages made hay, as did the numerous itinerant food and alcohol sellers, hustlers, card sharps and gamesters. As the early recorders of Ascot's history whispered, "As the night drew on, every form of vice was freely indulged in, and in a manner the mere repetition of which would shock our present tastes." Falling into the company of thieves or having your pocket picked were other situations where wealth could be redistributed. That assumed you had survived the journey to Windsor with your pocket intact, of course. On the road from London, Hounslow Heath was notorious for highwaymen.

In 1772 the Ascot meeting was officially titled "the Windsor and Ascot Heath Races" and its royalness was confirmed by the formality that the Duke of Gloucester, the Lord Warden of Windsor Forest, allowed it to take place. The year after it was "Windsor Races, Ascot Heath". Fortunately for racing, in the latter part of the eighteenth century George III improved facilities at Ascot and the Prince of Wales (later the Prince Regent and George IV) took a great interest in the sport. As Ascot week flourished, the town of Windsor prospered too, but with racing at Egham having resumed at 1770 there was little need or demand for any close to Windsor itself.

Neither Egham nor Windsor saw the great racehorse Eclipse run, even though he was foaled (during an eclipse) at the Duke of Cumberland's Cranbourne Lodge Stud in Windsor Great Park. Unbeaten in 18 races in as many months in 1769-70, he was sent to stud as there were no other rivals on the track for him to take on. There he became a tremendously successful sire and 95% of today's thoroughbreds are descended from him. The Eclipse Inn in Egham (now a restaurant) was named after him.

CHAPTER 2
THE MILITARY STEEPLECHASES

Thomas Coleman will always be remembered as the instigator of steeplechasing. He introduced the Great St Albans Steeplechase when he was proprietor of the Turf Hotel in the early 1830s. A few cross-country chases had been run before, where contestants rode whichever route they liked in order to get to the winning post first, which was found by aiming for a distant church steeple. These were generally private affairs with only a few horses. Coleman had the novel idea of starting and finishing a race at the same place, and advertising it as open to all comers. Better still was to have the race start close to his inn, where everyone assembled before and after.

Before that he had been employed to ride hunters in Windsor Great Park in order to qualify them for hunters' races at Ascot. (It would be wrong to assume that every race at Ascot since its inception was ultra-valuable; Sean Magee in his book Ascot: The History points out the standard of sport throughout the eighteenth century was quite moderate.) Coleman may well have been involved in three match races for officers run somewhere in the vicinity of Windsor in May 1821. The first two were on the flat, but the third was a one mile race with three five-feet high hurdles at intervals.

Steeplechasing caught on quickly and by 1840 there was an annual race or two in towns all over England. In December of that year there was one referred to as "Windsor", though they actually set off from Fyfield and finished at Oakley Green. The Brigade Steeplechase was confined to horses owned by officers of the Royal Household Brigade. There was a good size field of twelve, and Amazon won by fifty yards from Nimrod.

In all probability there had been other chases in and around Windsor in the 1830s; records are not comprehensive. It was typical in this early steeplechasing era for the venue to change from year to year. This meant the riders had to be shown round the course by the stewards before the race. This proved eventful in 1842 when one of the stewards tried to jump a ditch, and fell into it. It was so deep and muddy that once he had extricated himself onto terra firma, others had to help hold the horse's head up to prevent it from drowning. Lord Drumlanrig's The Cardinal won the race itself. He collected again next year when winning a consolation sweepstakes, and twice more in 1844. He was out of luck in a £20 race "for horses bona fide the property of members of White's, Crockford's, Brooks's, Boodle's, Croxton Park New Club, or of Officers on full pay, and ridden by members of the same" but two days later he carried 13 stone 3 pounds, most of which was his new owner Mr Langley, to win £50. That was in a match, in which both fell and refused at some stage of the contest. In the next race The Cardinal collected a much easier £30 by winning a walkover.

Changing the location wasn't the case with the race that was to become known as the Grand National, which soon settled at Aintree and one of whose early greats was the well-named Lottery, the winner in 1839. He won so many races up and down the country that some steeplechase promoters, fearful that he would scare off the opposition, framed the conditions of their races so that he would have to carry much more weight than his rivals. In one race at Horncastle the organisers went so far as to bar him from entering. He allegedly had a party trick (literally) whereby he would jump over a table where lunch had been laid out. At the end of a long career on the racetrack, he scored his 21st and final win at Windsor on 8 April 1844. Giving weight to all his opponents, the old boy won easily. The others didn't relish the fence guarded by a 17 foot wide brook that had to be jumped four times in the course of a race. Lottery's work was not yet done, for rumour has it that he wound up pulling a plough.

The Morning Post wrote about the races in glowing terms. "They have, from their high patronage and fashionable character at the outset, already attained a degree of celebrity in the sporting world as to rank among the first of chases in the country. At an early hour the town began to fill with holiday folk, and long before the hour appointed for starting, the roads to the course exhibited as much bustle and gaiety as an Ascot Cup day. The starting point was in a field at the back of Thompson's, a little to the right of the winning-post, which was judiciously placed on the high ground called Spital Hills, in front of the cavalry barracks, from whence nearly the whole distance could be traced." The King of the Belgians, no less, was present. Thompson was the manager of the meeting, possibly the farmer on whose land some of the course ran.

The 1847 Windsor steeplechase was won by Chandler, who was less renowned for his Grand National win in 1848 when aged 12 than for his record-breaking 39 foot leap during a race at Warwick. His jump, to clear an unfenced brook and four fallen rivals, was so amazing that spectators measured the distance of the hoof prints from the take-off to the landing side of the obstacle.

Meanwhile Windsor was still benefiting from the relative remoteness of Ascot. Railways reached Slough and Maidenhead in the 1830s, but it was further from there to Ascot than from Windsor. There was a description of "a long tail of pedestrians flowing through Windsor and Eton 'till nearly eleven o'clock at night, tired, wearied and depressed with the laborious bliss of the day ... The innkeepers made yesterday a very pretty thing out of it." The railway came to Windsor in 1849, but things changed in 1856, when the network spread at last to Ascot. Business in Windsor and other Berkshire towns diminished markedly now that racegoers could get from London to Ascot and back in a day, precluding the need for overnight stays.

Railways gave more opportunities for travel, and cheap fares for "race specials" fanned the flames. In 1867 there was even a special from Paddington to Windsor with horseboxes attached to cater for those going hunting with Her Majesty's Staghounds. New courses sprung up, especially around London, often initiated by publicans following the Thomas Coleman principle, and the ever-expanding railway network helped bring eager racegoers to them.

After 1849 there appear to be no Windsor steeplechases until a two-day meeting in November 1856, when the way The Serf's rider allowed him to lose by a neck "created considerable dissatisfaction." In an 1858 race Haphazard's rider Mr Crymes spent 20 minutes trying to get his mount to cross a fence which his two rivals also declined to jump. The RSPCA would not have approved of his methods, and when this obstacle was at last overcome Haphazard repeatedly refused at other fences and then proceeded to bolt off the course. Eventually he was persuaded to come back and complete the course and survived an objection, thus showing that sometimes Crymes does pay. The unfancied Half Caste fell in that day's Town Plate in his last run before being the subject of strong support for the Grand National and winning it.

The jumps course, periodically referred to as at Spital, was almost certainly to the east and south of the Combermere Barracks. There is still plenty of open space to the south. Extracts from contemporary newspaper reports below give tantalising glimpses of the approximate location of the races, and while at least one was clearly elsewhere, Spital was almost certainly the area where most of the Windsor steeplechases were held from the mid-1850s until 1874.

Apr 1857 the course crossed Bone Lane (roughly where Bolton Road is now).

Nov 1858 – the course is close to the Great Western Railway station

Nov 1860 - on the farms of Messrs Aldridge and Chater at Chippenham, but is also referred to as going from Eton Wick to Chippenham.

Apr 1861 - on reaching the fence on the brow of the hill near the hovel….

Apr 1863 - passing the Gardens …at the brook …Mr Higgins

rode a finish a circuit too soon, but carried on and won anyway on The Nabob. Nutcracker fell crossing the sewer, and broke his neck. (Yes, that's right, they had to jump the town's main drain. Woe betide anyone who fell in.)

1868 - Starting down the straight run in past the stand, over a fence into a field, round a large enclosure, back over the brook towards the stand, then sharp to the left — and away into the country.

The 1861 Windsor Open Steeplechase was graced by the most popular and probably the best French steeplechaser of the nineteenth century. Franc Picard was 15 by this time, and only succumbed by a neck to beat a horse ten years his junior after a four-mile slog, with eight other rivals failing to complete the course. Later that year he won his seventh Grand Steeple du Dieppe, after which he was retired, the winner of 46 of his 96 races.

The February 1864 Grand Annual and Military Steeplechases were a royal affair. The Prince of Wales was so pleased with Friday's races (having arrived after another Prince Edward, that of Saxe-Weimar) that he decided to come again on Saturday if his shooting party finished in time. The two main races were rearranged to take place at the end of the day for his benefit, but he didn't turn up, finding it "too fatiguing to be present".

A month later, another meeting on the flat and over hurdles, "got up entirely among amateurs" was held on "the lower meadows, at Clewer, about two and a half miles from Windsor." It's doubtful if this was the site of the current course, because "the charge of sixpence to the ground was evaded by hundreds, who got on the ground over the hedges." Nearly all the horse were hunters, hacks and cobs, but it was an enjoyable day for participants and spectators.

It was around this time that Queen Victoria had an unfortunate experience when watching the Windsor steeplechases from her carriage, which had been parked near one of the obstacles. The jockey in front, Ben Land, was heard to encourage his horse at the jump with extremely colourful language. Her Majesty was not amused and never attended another steeplechase meeting. Land concentrated on keeping his horse in front, but all his effort was for naught because he mistook a gatekeeper's box for the judge's box. Believing that it marked the winning post, he eased up after it and lost by a neck.

Even more farcical events ensued in 1868. The hard-pulling Bandoline was having his third race in two days, after a win and a fall, and in this particular event he was being partnered by a man having his first ride in public in the south of England, Wentworth Hope-Johnstone. Wenty, as he was known later in his distinguished amateur riding career, could not hold the free-running Bandoline and was coming up to a sharp left hand turn away from the stands and out into the country. Reggie Herbert, on the outside aboard the odds on Comberton, belatedly realised the other pair weren't going to make the turn, and after shouting at Wenty tried to force his way round the corner and take Bandoline with him. Though Wenty was oblivious to Herbert yelling at him, he managed to stay on track, but Comberton and Herbert didn't. They crashed into the carriages lining the course near the stands, the jockey landing on a table being laid for lunch. Cutlery and food flew everywhere. As Herbert told it, "To my astonishment when I was picked up and set on my legs, barring the shaking I felt none the worse; a greater surprise was to see an active bobby had got hold of Comberton, he also seemed none the worse and was trying to sample lettuce out of an overturned salad bowl. For the moment I had given up all idea of resuming the chase, but someone came running up shouting that the others had refused and one or two of 'em were in the main sewer, so the friendly bobby giving me a leg up I was soon in the saddle again and in hot pursuit, much to the surprise of Charley Kerr and several friends who had hurried down from the stand to pick up the pieces. After all it was the easiest of wins, for Bandoline had compounded at the next fence; I passed a couple of others stuck in the main drain, and overhauling the only remaining opponent at the last fence came away and won in a canter." Another version of the story states that once Herbert took off in pursuit, he went the wrong way and

WINDSOR—OVER THE ROPES.

Reggie Herbert and his horse fall into the picnickers

lost 300 yards before realising his error and retracing his steps.

On returning to the paddock, Herbert wondered why he was the recipient of an assortment of smiles, sniggers, and gasps, and belatedly realised that as a result of his tumble his breeches were not covering as much of him as they were meant to. After that he edged gingerly back to weigh in holding his saddle cloth strategically and keeping his back to the wall.

The Grand Military Gold Cup, the venue for which was selected one year at a time, came to Windsor in 1871. This marked the apogee of the Spital track's fortunes. The Sporting Times reported that "the course, a mile and a half in extent, has been improved by a new route being taken after the stand is passed, as the horses turn to the left instead of the right, and run back round a small loop, in which there are no abrupt turns as heretofore. The competitors are momentarily lost to view here by the occupants of the stand, but nearly every jump is to be seen." Mr Ray's Donato won for the Life Guards, ridden by Mr Pritchard. This historic race, first run in 1841, continued to do the rounds before settling in a permanent home at Sandown in the 1920s.

The 1873 military steeplechases were enlivened by two disqualifications, one because the winner had no pedigree certificate and the other because the first past the post had won a race worth more than £20, contravening the conditions of the race – a strangely common oversight in this era.

Disqualifications featured large in another race at Spital. Unusually, all four runners had got round without mishap. Three were fighting out the finish, so the rider of the fourth, who was well behind, pulled up and rode back to the paddock. When he went to congratulate the winner a few minutes later, he learned that he had been disqualified for going the wrong side of a post. He turned to the jockey on the second, only to hear that he had been disqualified too, for weighing in several pounds light. His jockey must have dropped the lead plates in his saddle that were necessary to bring him up to the required weight. Then he found the third had been disqualified as well. He had weighed in all right, but somehow he had neglected to weigh out before the race. The dumbfounded jockey on the fourth horse realised he could have won if he hadn't come off the track prematurely, but by now the judge had left his box, so nothing could be done. The race was declared void – nobody had won.

The 1874 meeting was marred by a serious accident to Lord Rossmore when unseated from the Marquess of Downshire's horse Harlequin in the Guards Cup. The rest of the meeting's civilian races were run but those confined to military personnel were called off. Rossmore lingered near death's door for a few weeks before he succumbed. Reginald Herbert spoke movingly of his fellow jockey. "One of the best fellows that ever drew breath met his death riding over this same course, and that was poor Rossmore. I call to mind we travelled down from Paddington together overflowing with la joie de vivre, and two hours later I was under a fence holding up his head whilst the life ebbed slowly out of him. I've never come across a more loveable nature than his, nor has any one else, or I'm much mistaken." Rossmore who was only 22, had taken a severe fall at the same course three years earlier. It became a double tragedy with the death of Downshire at about the same time. He was only 30, but had been ill for some time and the shock of hearing about Rossmore's fall sent him into a decline from which he could not recover.

This signalled the end of the Windsor military steeplechases, which had seen more than its fair share of equine fatalities and injured jockeys over the years. It was understandable that Colonel Charles Rivers Bulkeley, their organiser for 18 years, did not wish to arrange a meeting in 1875. Bulkeley had ridden as "Mr Charles" in the early 60s, winning a steeplechase at one of the rare meetings at Chertsey (they were held in 1845, 1856 and 1864-67). There were plenty of other courses that could host military meetings.

There were a couple of jump meetings in the first part of 1876, one with a few military races and one for galloways (ponies). The other was a meeting of the Road Club, an aristocratic gathering confined to horses owned and ridden by its members. The latter was at "the Ham, Old Windsor, where the old military steeplechases were", but surely not on the same very testing course that their predecessors used. Four of the six events were matches and one of the others had just two runners.

CHAPTER THREE
JOHN FRAIL

We owe the creation of Windsor racecourse to John Frail, a Shrewsbury man born in 1804. Though he left school aged 13 unable to read or write (so he claimed in later life) in order to become a barber, he was intelligent and astute – so much so that he quickly became one of the most prominent people in the town and its civic affairs. For many years he was the most prominent Conservative in the area.

In the middle of the nineteenth century the electorate consisted only of gentlemen who owned property above a certain value. In some constituencies this meant the number of voters was only in the hundreds. Prospective MPs for the two parties, Conservative and Whigs (i.e. Liberals) resorted to bribery frequently, and though that was technically illegal one had to be unusually flagrant to be prosecuted. Cash incentives were politely known as “golden spurs”. Frail was one of a trio called The Knot who ran the Conservative party in Shrewsbury, which meant selecting candidates and organising campaigns to get them elected – hence his title of “election agent”. The town was entitled to return two MPs. Benjamin Disraeli was one of those elected in 1841, and he of course went on to be Prime Minister twice.

Frail was energetic and good at his job, and therefore was loathed by his political opponents. He had contacts with the party headquarters in London. He was a fluent speaker and a talented singer, often being called on to perform at official functions. However, there were some notable lapses in taste, such as the occasion when all the respectable ladies present walked out on hearing him sing a particularly coarse ditty. Another time he vehemently abused a fellow councillor, calling him “a blasted two-faced liar, a damnation bloody liar, a blasted two-faced scoundrel and a rotten rogue”.

He revived the ailing Shrewsbury racecourse to great effect, being appointed Clerk of the Course in 1843. To begin with only nine horses were entered for its autumn meeting, but he soon multiplied that many times over. Even his political opponents recognised his organisational ability, and there were obviously several prominent local individuals who had a legitimate interest in both racing and politics. At the other end of the spectrum, Frail also succeeded in making the races popular with the general public.

Frail gradually built up a controlling interest in the Racecourse Company and for a time in the 1850s and 60s he was involved with Ludlow races too. In his role as an election agent he helped out the Conservatives there when the Whigs brought in some roughs to threaten key locals. He did this by bringing in his own heavy mob. He also knew a man whose crimes were in a different league, William Palmer of Rugeley.

Palmer was a racing man and, like many others, his betting led him into debt. Several of Palmer's family and friends died sudden agonising deaths soon after he had taken out life assurance policies on them. Following the demise of his friend John Cook after the 1855 Shrewsbury races he was tried for murder and hanged. We cannot be sure how many people he sent to an early grave. The case made front-page headlines and the townspeople of Rugeley were so horrified by Palmer's association with the town they attempted to have it renamed.

In later years Frail would relate how when staying at a Newmarket hotel he and Palmer had been given a double room. With £3,000 cash in his pocket, and knowing the suspicions beginning to float around Palmer, Frail locked him out of the room and ignored his banging on the door wanting to get in. He had the room to himself that night. It makes a good story, but the likelihood of a man like Frail carrying that much cash (today's equivalent value is £300,000) casts doubt on its veracity. So does the fact that he told another version in which the hotel was in Liverpool, and Palmer's eyes supposedly lit up when before going down to breakfast he saw Frail take the money out of its hiding place under the pillow.

Frail's underhand tactics in politics were inevitably repeated in racing. He had interests in horses, though he was not necessarily the formal owner. In 1852 he was alleged to have instructed a trainer to ensure that his horse did not win a heat of the Members' Plate. There were other disputes in 1856-57 about his role as handicapper, where it was easy to favour one's racehorse-owning friends by giving their horses less weight to carry than their form warranted. As some sceptics observed when a string of heavily-backed favourites won, the handicaps weren't always masterpieces.

In Sixty Years on the Turf, written by George Hodgman at the end of the nineteenth century, we're told a plausible story about Frail showing he wasn't reticent about his origins and that he was a dangerous man to cross. When appearing in the witness box in a Parliamentary bribery case, the prosecutor launched into him.

"What is your name?"
"John Frail."
"What are you?"
"A barber at Shrewsbury."
"Ah, John Frail! According to my instructions a very frail man! Have you been long at Shrewsbury?"

Frail didn't appreciate the feeble attempt at humour at his expense. "Yes. Nearly all my life, and I know you, and you should have known me. I shaved you many times at Shrewsbury when you were courting two sisters."

Frail's examination was quickly brought to an end.

Notwithstanding his darker side, Frail was a skilful administrator and innovator. He introduced the system whereby owners were required to pay a fee to the Clerk of the Course in order to enter their horse in a race. Having increased the number of runners at Shrewsbury by framing attractive races and improving the racecourse and its facilities, this method of payment suited him more than a flat fee. This practice soon extended to other officials, so that in addition the Clerk of the Scales was paid a fee per runner, and the stakeholder was paid a percentage of the stakes.

Referring to Shrewsbury's autumn meeting that marked the culmination of the flat racing season, The Times said, "We are ignorant of the secret that Mr John Frail possesses in being able to tempt from their homes and firesides at this season of the year the concourse of people who have filled the hotels and lodgings of Shrewsbury .... Beds are at a premium and upwards of 200 horses have already arrived." The meeting was scheduled to run from Monday to Thursday but Frail put on extra races on Friday, and if need be Saturday, if there was demand from the vast array of owners.

Hodgman remarked that "some funny things have been done at Shrewsbury, particularly at the Autumn Meeting" and the penultimate day of the 1862 season was a case in point. Four Turf regulars had lost most of their betting money and were casting around for ways to get some of it back. They hit upon the idea of creating an extra race on the final day just for themselves. They would enter their own horses, arrange the result between them in advance, square it with their jockeys and bet accordingly. They put the proposition for an extra race to Frail, who no doubt made something out of it for himself. Unfortunately, even though the deadline for entries was four o'clock on the day that the extra race was devised, somebody else entered their horse for it too. This was "a wretched bad horse" called Tom Sayers.

The conspirators thought it over and decided that they would let Tom Sayers win. One of them encouraged the top jockey George Fordham to seek the ride, and when he approached the unsuspecting owner Mr Priestley his offer was accepted gratefully. By the time the field had reached the start £1,000 had been bet on his horse by the collaborators. Tom Sayers then refused to race, but the other riders pretended it was a false start and returned to the starting area. (Was the starter in on the plot anyway?) When they did get away successfully, Fordham was allowed to take the lead, get a position on the rail, and stay in front. Luckily autumnal fogginess blurred the antics of the riders of the chasing quartet who had to appear to make an effort. Tom Sayers crawled past the winning post three quarters of a length in front. The owners of the losers collected £2,500 from their bets on the winner.

Frail saw the growth in speculative racecourse ventures, especially in the south east, and decided there were profits to be made by setting up a new course himself. His beady eye was on the faltering fortunes of the Egham meeting, where the management and the Clerk of the Course had fallen out. In Egham Races 1734-1884 Maurice E Lord states that "by the latter part of the 1860s it was clear that all was not as it should be in the control of petty crime at the meeting and by 1867 respectable spectators had to take refuge in the stands to avoid being subject to all manner of indignities." Given Frail's strong-arm electioneering tactics one wonders if the hooligans had been given an incentive to prey on Egham.

In December 1864 he, John Jenner Saltmarsh, a man well known in racing circles, and another crony, Richard Pearse, agreed to form a partnership to find and run a racecourse near London. Saltmarsh was to look out for a suitable venue and he soon found some land at Clewer, a mile west of Windsor. Frail went to inspect the flat, fertile farmland. He liked what he saw. The fact that much of its boundary was formed by the river Thames, with the rest bordered by a tributary, meant natural barriers would prevent people getting in for nothing.

Though they had no formal written partnership, the three men agreed that Saltmarsh and Frail would approach the owners of the land and its tenant. The land was owned by the local MP, William Vansittart, and solicitor George Henry Long, trustees for the late Arthur Vansittart, the beneficiary of the land's enclosure around 1818. They in turn leased it to farmer John Gristwood. Saltmarsh asked Frail's elder son, Charles Simpson Frail, to act on his behalf. The Frails went so far as to announce dates in mid-August 1865 for the first race meeting. They became available when Oxford was forced to give up its fixture owing to a legal dispute between its organisers, the Town Council and the Freemen of the City.

They were undeterred by the appearance of a new steeplechase meeting near Datchet scheduled for February of that year. A nearby jumps meeting did not in itself represent competition for the Frails' flat-only affair, but the danger was that Datchet was arranged by John

Frederick Verrall. He was the energetic instigator and organiser of several suburban meetings and if Datchet took off Verrall might try to add flat racing to the programme.

The meeting was deferred three weeks due to frost. Verrall curried favour with the soldiers stationed locally by offering them reduced price admission. Its first day went well, but the second had just five races, including two sellers (one of which was won by Donkey) and a match. There were reports of gentlemen being mugged and pickpocketed at the railway station. Possibly Verrall saw richer pickings elsewhere, for no further National Hunt meetings took place at Datchet.

Negotiations over Clewer went well and an agreement to sell was soon reached, although Pearse decided to withdraw from the project. Saltmarsh agreed with John Frail that they should be sole lessees and equal partners, and he told Charles to carry on, leaving the matter in his hands. However, plans for an August meeting were abandoned as Oxford was, after all, able to race on its original dates.

In June 1865 Saltmarsh was incensed to read that a lease of 160 acres of land at Clewer had been prepared and that race meetings were planned in the spring and summer to follow those at Ascot. That year was the first time Ascot had held a meeting in the spring in addition to the long-established Royal meeting in June. It had been so successful they planned to repeat the exercise. Frail's plan was to make Windsor the next port of call for all the Turfites who thronged to Ascot.

Bell's Life went on to report that, "Mr John Frail has been entrusted with the management and he has induced the following noblemen to act as Stewards: The Duke of Beaufort, the Duke of Newcastle, the Marquess of Hastings, the Marquess of Aylesbury, the Earl of Westmorland, the Earl of Stamford, Earl Poulett, Lord Bateman. With such distinguished and influential names, and the Newmarket staff as officials a good meeting can scarcely fail to be the result. A permanent and commodious grandstand is about to be erected forthwith from the design of Mr J F Clark." The Berkshire Chronicle was in no doubt; "in these days, when everybody is racing mad, the speculation is certain to be a remunerative one."

Saltmarsh discovered that Charles Frail had drawn up the Clewer lease making no reference to him. John Frail was the sole lessee. The freeholders had been told that the other partners had given up their interest in the matter. Saltmarsh demanded an explanation and Charles retorted by saying he did not recognise the legitimacy of his claims.

The aggrieved Saltmarsh found a lawyer who said he had a case against John Frail for a half share of the lease and the racecourse, which was by now under construction. He threatened to take Charles to court regarding his failure to act properly on his behalf.

The case of Saltmarsh versus Frail started its progression through the Court of Queen's Bench at Westminster in January 1866. Evidence emerged gradually, in the form of a series of written questions and answers from each side punctuated by occasional hearings.

Not surprisingly, the Frails' version of events differed significantly from that of Saltmarsh. John Frail claimed that as long ago as December 1863 he had been advised by James Dally, a trainer and horse dealer based in Old Windsor, that there was land at Clewer that would do for a racecourse. He agreed that Saltmarsh mentioned Clewer was suitable a year later but denied that there was any formal arrangement for him to scout for likely sites. Frail also cast doubt on the notion that Dally's site and Saltmarsh's were exactly the same. In January 1865 a proposed Heads of Agreement was drawn up – a non-binding document that precedes a formal contract – which specified how much each of four shareholders should deposit in a bank account. That quartet consisted of John Frail, Richard Pearse, Saltmarsh and a man called Valentine Wright. Frail was to keep all the income from owners who paid to enter their horses, and from gate money; profits would be divided among the shareholders. Although the Heads of Agreement was approved, it was not signed. Nevertheless at least one local newspaper reported that a new racecourse was being established on Rays Meadow, near Clewer.

According to Frail, next month Saltmarsh told him he could not raise the money to deposit his share and asked if he would lend it to him. Frail refused, at which point Saltmarsh said he would have nothing more to do with the scheme. Charles, who regularly acted as solicitor for his father, denied that he was employed by Saltmarsh. Indeed, the nature of the project made it undesirable for him to do so. Perhaps with tongue in cheek, he stated that Saltmarsh was "an acute man of business, fully competent to protect his own interests; I never gave him any advice as a solicitor about this."

Pearse and Wright dropped out independently, probably because the Frails realised they needed more of the land at Clewer than they first envisaged. Either that or the financial aspects were too onerous or risky for their liking. Frail could afford to go it alone, and the Clewer people were willing to negotiate with him.

Saltmarsh sounded out Frail again in April, but Frail replied that he wouldn't have him as a partner. However, he offered to withdraw from the whole project if the Clewer landowners and Saltmarsh agreed terms. That was an empty offer, seeing as Saltmarsh was hard up.

In August 1865 a 21 year lease was agreed whereby Frail would pay £370 per annum rent for Clewer (which would increase if there were more than two meetings a year) and a substantial permanent grandstand costing at least £500 would be built within the next three years. Frail promptly advertised for tenders to build the new stand.

Once Saltmarsh embarked on his legal action the Frails encountered other problems. Floods in February 1866 were so bad that the first race meeting, scheduled for 22 and 23 March, had to be postponed well in advance. In a letter to the Sporting Life Saltmarsh commented on this with ponderous humour, saying that Frail should have referred to a "Saltmarsh" instead of "wet marshes" being the problem. Then the Ascot spring meeting failed miserably, and in a complete volte-face the prevailing opinion was that it would not be revived. That torpedoed the idea of a money-spinning meeting at Windsor directly afterwards.

A good crowd was in attendance on Tuesday 5 June 1866 for the long-delayed inaugural meeting. It was a good date to have, being the day after Founders' Day across the river at Eton, which brought illustrious parents to the area. The Prince of Wales was expected to attend, but more serious business reviewing troops at Colchester prevented him from doing so. At least the Jockey Club's senior handicapper Admiral Rous was there, as were Henry Chaplin and the Marquess of Hastings, rivals for the love of Lady Florence Paget. (Although engaged to Chaplin, while out shopping for her wedding she notoriously eloped with Hastings, a story which gained even more spice as Hastings continually opposed Chaplin's horse Hermit in the betting for the Derby. Hermit won, Hastings lost a lot of money, and died aged 26 a year later.) The Members' stand, described as "a convenient and elegant looking brick building, with an extensive range of wooden steps in front". In the main Tattersalls' enclosure there was a grandstand capable of accommodating 2,000 people. The design of the stands and the administration drew general praise, helped by Frail ensuring that needs of the press well catered for and thereby encouraging favourable comment. Nevertheless he was regarded with understandable suspicion by some on the Turf, for as The Era commented, "Mr Frail must be a clever man from the number of enemies he has."

There was no figure of eight like we know today; the course then was shaped like a 6. There was no jumping circuit (although very occasionally a hurdle race or a race on the flat for hunters would be run). The longest race was one mile and five furlongs, in which runners started near the winning post and ran away from the stands, forking left at the intersection and taking the far loop clockwise. That loop was bigger than the one we know today, with runners joining the straight course much closer to the six furlong start.

A very full day was planned, with nine events scheduled. To modern eyes there was a certain monotony about the proceedings, the race distances being

4f 4f 4f 1m5f 5f 6f 4f 4f 6f

This diet was common in this era, with the fashion having swung from stamina-laden events to the other extreme. This would remain the case until the late 1870s, when the Jockey Club decreed that at least half the day's prize money should be devoted to races of a mile or more.

John Frail

Twelve two-year-olds went down to the start for the first race, run over half a mile and worth £50 to the winner. After a false start the Chaplin-owned Satyr, the 4/1 second favourite, strolled in three lengths ahead. George Fordham was the winning jockey. He was champion 14 times in the third quarter of the nineteenth century and was by far the most successful jockey of the Victorian era until Fred Archer came along.

Racegoers without the necessary stamina didn't miss much if they left early; the eighth race was a walkover and the ninth race, a private match, was called off by mutual consent. Two winners, Indian Star and an unnamed colt by Tadmor, were owned by Lord Westmorland, one of the stewards, and ridden by Sam Kenyon, who this year would be champion jockey. Harvey Covey also rode a double. Mr Wyatt's Jupiter won the big race, the £150 Windsor Summer Handicap.

Another large crowd was drawn to the Rays on Wednesday afternoon, with another nine-race programme to enjoy. Indian Star won again for the same owner and jockey. Lord Westmorland had yet another success with Practitioner. Count de Lagrange's Dragon, by taking the Royal Stakes over five furlongs, earned a quote of 25/1 for the 1867 Derby, fifty weeks in the future.

Court hearings in the Saltmarsh case dragged on until the middle of 1867 before petering out. The nature of its conclusion is unclear. Either the Frails made a private out of court settlement to get Saltmarsh to drop the matter, or he ran out of cash or legal arguments to pursue it any further. What is certain is that John Frail emerged as the sole leaseholder of the racecourse.

Saltmarsh attracted controversy regularly and was a slippery customer, but was not in the same league as the Frails. In 1864, a year in which he bought and sold several racehorses – quite possibly on behalf of others – his Confusion was reported in Bell's Life as being awarded the Worthing Cup as a result of a steward's enquiry. The apostrophe there is correct, for Lord Westmorland was the only steward to deliberate on the matter, because another who was present had an interest in the case and had to stand aside. However, having only one steward for an enquiry contravenes the rules of racing. Saltmarsh knew the rule book, for he was a steward at the Hendon race meeting. Confusion had finished third in the race, but Saltmarsh had objected to the first two for taking the wrong course and additionally claimed the winner should be disqualified because one owner could not have two horses running in this particular race. To complicate things further, the Clerk of the Course then wrote to Bell's Life to say that he had not sent in a report about Confusion's promotion and it was a forgery.

In 1865 Saltmarsh lost a court case where he had disputed liability for a £100 debt. He was also caught up in a case of disputed ownership. A Baron Molembaix acquired a horse with the unfortunate name of Piggy Wiggy. He asked his trainer-jockey, Pickett, to look after him and as a result the horse was sent to Barrett's livery yard in Bayswater. The Baron went abroad, and without his knowledge Pickett ran the horse in a selling race at Reading, where Saltmarsh bought him. He sent Piggy Wiggy back to Barrett's yard for safe keeping, who refused to hand the horse over to Molembaix when he claimed it. A court awarded the Baron damages of £100 against Barrett, although Pickett seems to be more at fault. Molembaix eventually managed to buy Piggy Wiggy back. This kind of horse trading was typical of the racing world of the nineteenth century.

A few years after his abortive involvement with Windsor

Saltmarsh was the landlord of the Gray's Inn Tavern when a victim of theft was plied with drink and cigars before being robbed. The boot was on the other foot when, in another of his properties, he discovered a servant with 27 pairs of gloves in her possession, stolen from her previous employer. In 1872, he was one of the defendants in a prosecution taken out by his wife. Despite a life of turmoil and conflict he lived till he was 86, dying in 1896.

Meanwhile the Frails prospered and avoided controversy. In the 1870s the dodgy deals were gradually fading into the past and the success of Shrewsbury and Windsor made the proprietors of other courses look towards the Frails, and wonder if they could do the same for them. Though the Jockey Club began to disallow the same individual holding multiple roles at a single course, to prevent conflicts of interest, where a family was involved fathers, sons and brothers (and it was only ever men) could split the duties between themselves. The result was that a few families, such as the Verralls and the Frails, acquired control of several courses' operations.

John Frail had delayed expanding his empire until his oldest son, Charles, was ready to be take over some of the work. Charles, born in 1836, trained as a solicitor and when he was appointed as Coroner in his home town in 1861 he became the youngest holder of such a post in England. Once Windsor races were established Charles and the younger son John Ernest were increasingly concerned with racing business. Thus began a three-generation empire of racecourse officials, of increasing respectability.

Frail senior was like some other racing personalities of the nineteenth century whose dubious reputations were overlooked in their later years as they confined themselves to more legitimate pursuits. He was brought in to help run a big new course at Bristol. The Prince of Wales was present for the inaugural meeting in March 1873, whose centrepiece was the peripatetic National Hunt Chase, a race that was second in importance only to the Grand National. The day went well, and Frail was presented to the royal visitor. He declared his hope that the Prince might live long and prosper, and that he and his dynasty might survive "all Radicals, Fenians, and revolutionary thieves for a thousand years."

Frail saw the potential for a rival to the Grand National to be staged in the relatively undeveloped (in racing terms) west of England and devised a valuable event called the Royal Chase for Bristol's 1874 meeting. Hopes that the Prince of Wales might return were dashed at the last minute. In spite of all the money spent on the course and lavish prize money, it was too expensive to maintain. The Frails, no doubt seeing the writing on the wall, ended their participation in 1877 and the track closed in 1880.

Old John, who had achieved the much-coveted office of mayor of Shrewsbury in 1878, died of bronchitis the year after. His sons carried on the business of administering Windsor and their other courses. The Shrewsbury racecourse closed in 1884, when the lease expired, but by then they were running Northampton, Huntingdon and Manchester.

CHAPTER FOUR
RACING BECOMES ESTABLISHED

Two meetings were planned for Windsor's second year in 1867, but in a frustrating repetition of bad luck, the spring fixture was abandoned again due to floods. However, good weather helped the summer meeting draw a crowd "greatly in excess of last year" for eight and nine race programmes. The star of the show was the Oaks winner of two years before, Regalia, who won the Windsor Summer Handicap in a canter despite having three hard races at Royal Ascot the previous week over distances between one mile and two and a half; she was unplaced in the Hunt Cup and second in the Queen's Vase and the Gold Cup.

The Royal meeting continued to bring people into Windsor, not to universal satisfaction. A disgruntled resident complained about a house used as a gambling den open during Ascot week that carried on through the following Windsor race meeting. He claimed the police knew about it and were failing in their duty to close it down.

The Frails were undoubtedly aiming at quantity rather than quality, as it was futile to compete with Ascot. Occasionally a good horse was entered, such as Prince Charlie, who had won all of his ten races in 1873. His first run the year after was in the Windsor Stand Cup, and he won that too before being aimed at better things.

In the second half of the 1870s new courses opened at Sandown and Kempton. They aspired to the top end of the market, which further reinforced Windsor's position as a purveyor of bread-and-butter racing in a pleasant setting. That model has been in operation ever since, with a few dramatic exceptions, as we shall see later. A motley collection of courses in the London suburbs, generally thought to be public nuisances and hotbeds of chicanery, closed down at about the same time. This was the case with minor Berkshire flat racing venues such as Reading and Abingdon too; they could not afford to continue without falling foul of increasing Jockey Club regulation.

Windsor gradually obtained more fixtures. First an August meeting; then in 1874 it revived the spring meeting. By taking in the ground at the rear of the paddock (which was then opposite the winning post) a two-mile course was formed for a Hunters Stakes and a handicap hurdle. A July meeting was added in 1882.

Dry summers did make for a drastic reduction in field sizes, as in June 1875 when the first and last races were walkovers, a £200 race attracted only three horses and the £300 Royal Cup was only prevented from being a walkover due to the eleventh-hour arrival of a second runner. At the other extreme, flooding occurred frequently but not usually at times that affected racing. Nevertheless parts of the course were under water in June and August 1879, February and October 1880, January, February and November 1881. That was an unusually bad spell, but nobody put it down to climate change.

In keeping with recent trends elsewhere, from 1881 the course was fenced off so that all racegoers had to pay to get a sight of the action, rather than just those who patronised the stands and the area immediately around.

One lively bunch of prospective customers lay a mile or so over the river in Eton College. For generations there was a battle of wits between scholars and masters, the former eager to get to the races and the latter keen to prevent them.

Though the fabulously wealthy Lord Barrymore first graced the Turf officially in 1789, he is sure to have sampled Ascot informally prior to that while he was still at Eton. One night he and another boy escaped from their rooms and went round all the pubs in Windsor, quietly swapping all their inn signs round. Barrymore's pranks and his love of carousing led him to a premature sticky end; by 1793 he'd got through £300,000 (about £40 million today), when he was accidentally shot and killed by his servant.

The first challenge for the young Etonian racing fan was the problem of the roll-call ("Absence") at two o'clock. The obvious solution was to get a friend to answer your name for you boldly while standing in the middle of a crowd of ideally-slightly taller boys. A softly-spoken or hesitant call might arouse the master's suspicions and if he asked the boy to step forward and recognised he was an impostor, both he and the absentee were in trouble.

The final challenge was to get back to Eton in time for the six o'clock roll call. Many ran to Ascot and back. Getting a lift was better, and with the help of Old Etonians or older brothers the journey was easier still. A particularly resourceful half-dozen disguised themselves as blacked-up travelling minstrels and drove there and back unchallenged.

On another occasion almost a hundred of them were nabbed on the way home. They were given "lines" as a punishment, namely writing out a hundred lines of a Greek poem each day.

One of them, the future trainer the Honourable George Lambton, wistfully recalled that the only time he managed to get one over on authority was when his indolent master failed to notice he hadn't submitted his lines. A later review of his scholastic shortcomings lamented, "At Eton he was rather too near Ascot, and at Cambridge rather too near Newmarket." His academic failures didn't stop him training twelve classic winners, being the leading trainer twice, and writing one of the best racing autobiographies ever, Men and Horses I Have Known.

The Spital jumps course and Rays Meadow provided more racegoing opportunities and were much closer to Eton. Boys were forbidden from being on the Windsor side of the river on race days, but it is a very short swim from the "Athens" riverbank on the north side of the river from the back straight. Ordinarily Athens was an authorised bathing place for Eton boys, though decorum required that any in a state of undress should ensure they concealed themselves if boats containing ladies approached. It's said that a future Steward of the Jockey Club used to swim across to the racecourse with his clothes balanced on his head.

When masters kept watch on the river absconding boys had to go to Windsor races via the town, though by the early part of the twentieth century older boys were getting considerably more daring.

Riding a finish in 1896; note the whip action (Racing Illustrated/courtesy of Tim Cox)

More scenes from 1896 (Racing Illustrated/courtesy of Tim Cox)

They managed to get to Kempton, Sandown and Hurst Park as well. They had to raise cash first to be able to afford a room at the White Hart in Windsor to change clothes, hiring transport to and from their destination, entrance to the course itself and betting money.

There had always been Windsor folk happy to help the boys by taking bets, giving tips or lending money. In his autobiography Racing From Within Frank Atherton Brown listed seven bookies they could choose from; one of the boys who boarded, Trottie the cabman who always parked near the school between 12 and 1, "three local pros as safe as the Bank of England," old Solomon in the High Street hatters, and mine host at Tap, an unofficial yet long-established bar for older boys. After the Second World War one of the boys acted as a runner for the town bookmaker, relaying bets and winnings. This was John Bingham, who later inherited the title of Lord Lucan.

The races were, by virtue of their increasing frequency, less of a special occasion for the people of Windsor. Combined with the need to pay to go in, it was becoming more of a commercial event laid on for the benefit of those people for whom racing was their chief occupation. The Sporting Times of 14 July 1883 described it thus. "For some reason or other the inhabitants of Windsor keep aloof from the races. They lounge about the streets, stare at their London visitors from their doors and windows, loaf about the pothouses, but never plank down their money and support Messrs Frail's meeting. The half-dollar charged for admission has, no doubt, something to do with their abstention from the Rays; but in the old shilling days not many more persons were present, and, with the exception of one drag full of officers, not a single Windsor warrior was to be seen."

One reason why locals may have kept clear that year was the alleged attack in March on Lady Florence Dixie about half a mile past the entrance to the racecourse. She claimed she was set upon by two men dressed as women, armed with a dagger. According to her confused account she fought them off with the aid of her St Bernard. Almost immediately the press stated their belief that no attack had taken place. They regarded her as a publicity-seeker. She was talented but wayward; an explorer, travel writer, would-be politician and, worst of all, a feminist, a quality that did not endear her to the Establishment. Four years earlier her pet jaguar killed some deer in Windsor Great Park, which wouldn't have endeared her to the locals either.

Lady Florence was born into the talented but colourful Queensberry family. Her father, the 8th Marquess, apparently committed suicide. Her twin brother cut his own throat. Another brother, the 9th Marquess, devised the set of rules for boxing known as the Queensberry Rules, but later found fame of a less welcome sort by branding Oscar Wilde a "somdomite", one of the most notable misspellings in history. This was in retaliation for the famous author's affair with his son. Wilde sued for libel and lost, after which he was convicted of gross indecency and sent to prison. Lady Florence's husband lost their main family home due to his unsuccessful betting on the horses.

Nobody was ever charged with the supposed crime. Respectable local people were certainly deterred by the growing number of disreputable characters and career criminals that were part of the racing circus and descended on each town that hosted a meeting. A publican who was busy with the extra raceday custom didn't have time to bank the takings and settled for putting almost £100 in a cashbox and leaving it in a locked drawer in an upstairs bedroom. That evening a gang organised a phoney dispute in the bar and while this charade diverted everyone's attention their confederates got into the bedroom via an outhouse roof and stole the cash. The publican didn't realise he had been robbed until after closing time, when the gang had long gone.

There was a strange doublethink for many years that it was only to be expected that if you went racing, you would be robbed unless you were a regular or exercised basic common sense, i.e. not flashing large amounts of cash, keeping your valuables out of sight or better still at home, and avoiding games of chance. Some crooks were enterprising in their way. One stood between the payment booth and the entrance to the enclosures saying "Tickets, gentlemen," and at least one man gave his ticket to the miscreant. He was caught, but without the racegoer's testimony in court he was let off. A punter holding his winning ticket up to a bookie in order to be paid out had it snatched from him. An ex-constable apprehended the culprit when he tried the same thing later; his first victim had recognised him and pointed him out. He was convicted and sentenced to two months' hard labour.

These hazards were just as prevalent on the way to the track. Card games on trains were obvious pitfalls, and so could be the friendly stranger in an age when people were more trusting or naïve than they are now. A visitor from South America, Hugh Blunt, got talking to a Mr Brotzell on the race train from Paddington. At the races they had a few drinks and Brotzell introduced Blunt to a man called Johnson who supposedly had inside information. Blunt allowed Johnson to bet for him and at the end of the unsuccessful day gave him a cheque for £60 to cover his losses. The next day another £15 in cash went the same way before a detective overheard what was going on. Brotzell was arrested and sentenced to nine months in prison. Fortunately Blunt was able to stop the cheque and didn't lose all his money.

Racecourse managers washed their hands of all responsibility for those outside events and got away with it. This was summed up by the Slough Observer in the mid-1880s thus: "Windsor races were held on Thursday and Friday, and there was the customary gathering of bullies, thieves, welchers, pickpockets, low betting-men, and other hawks and sharks, from the metropolis." Yet the same report went on to say, "The management was excellent."

In 1892 "Prince Theodore", who claimed to be the son of the King of Abyssinia, was found guilty of threatening behaviour towards Robert Jacobs at Windsor races. The court heard Theodore say in distinctly unprincely terms that "he would do for Jacobs even if he had to swing for it". The Prince often appeared in court for relatively minor offences and was usually able to charm magistrates into treating him leniently. Not this time; he was sent to prison for three months.

After racing at Windsor one afternoon in 1894 bookmaker Lancelot Logan was viciously attacked by a gang of hooligans, though they stole nothing. Logan offered a reward of £500 for the conviction of whoever instigated the assault. Nothing came of it publicly, where the motivation was dismissed as "malice". That same day one of the senior stewards, Sir George Chetwynd, nearly lost his watch and chain to more conventional pickpockets when he hailed a cab. Chetwynd had married Lady Florence Paget after the premature demise of her first husband, the Marquess of Hastings. Lady Florence was to die in Long Walk House near Windsor Castle in 1907.

In December 1914 after a Windsor race meeting there was an argument at the station between race gang members; George Morton threatened James O'Neill with a knife. When their train stopped at Clapham Junction Morton went along the platform looking for O'Neill. Spotting Morton, O'Neill jumped him and in the fracas Morton was fatally stabbed with his own knife. O'Neill, described by police as "a dangerous criminal and an associate of expert thieves", was convicted of manslaughter and sentenced to seven years in jail. It was probably six of one and half a dozen of the other. The only saving grace about race gang warfare was that they usually killed or maimed each other.

Problems could arise when a race meeting clashed with another important event in the town. On 20 June 1908 a royal garden party was scheduled on the same day as Windsor races. Although the timing of the races was brought forward in order for them to have caught their trains back home before guests returned from the Castle, it began to rain and people left the garden party earlier than expected. When they arrived at the station, dressed up to the nines, they got mixed up with the racing crowd and the light-fingered men who preyed on crowds. Many lost their tiepins and watches.

The top flat race jockeys rode at Windsor, thanks at first to its proximity to Ascot and later due to the increasing concentration of meetings near London. In those days jockeys were allowed to bet, and did so with alacrity, not just on their own mounts but also those of their opponents. Despite the enormous scope for chicanery some were honourable about it. Fred Archer was asked to ride an unfancied tearaway called Westwood in a race at Windsor, and he agreed, though he added that he was going to bet £500 on Domino, another runner in

ROYAL WINDSOR RACE CLUB

ROYAL WINDSOR

AUGUST MEETING.

SECOND DAY,

Friday, August 12th, 1898.

STEWARDS:

Sir R. WILMOT, Bart. Sir JOHN THURSBY, Bart.
Hon. C. HOWARD. C. J. MERRY, Esq.
Captain HOMFRAY. H. HUNGERFORD, Esq.
Major JOICEY.

Mr. A. Coventry, Starter.
Mr. Lawley, Judge. Mr. Dawkins, Handicapper.
Mr. C. Frail, Jun., Clerk of the Scales.
Messrs. Frail, 52, Maddox Street, London, W.,
Clerks of the Races and Stakeholders.

PRICE SIXPENCE.

WINDSOR
OXLEY AND SON, PRINTERS (BY AUTHORITY), HIGH STREET.

that race. In the race, he tried his utmost and Westwood beat the subject of his bet by a neck. Much the same thing happened with Tom Cannon, the 1872 champion jockey and rider of 13 classic winners, who was brought up in Eton. He rode Lady Atholstone to win by a head at Windsor despite having bet on the runner-up. Unlike Archer, he only had £20 on.

Another time when in the Windsor paddock Archer had been impressed by Cohort, one of his rivals. Just before taking his own horse out onto the course he whispered to his horse's groom to tell a friend of his to put £200 on. Cohort won at 6/1. Knowing Archer, the groom would have been given a present for performing that little errand. In August 1874 paddock watchers noticed a horse called Lincoln being given half a bottle of whisky by his trainer "to assist his temper" before winning easily. Such stimulation wasn't against the rules.

A less honourable jockey was Robert Wyatt, whose effort, or rather lack of effort on Nougat that day caught the eye. Before the four-horse Welter Stakes, his odds had drifted alarmingly, from evens to 5/1. The favourite Carlos made all the running and beat Nougat by a length.

The conscientious Henry Chaplin led the stewards' enquiry. When he found that Carlos and Nougat were due to run again the next day, he instructed both their jockeys to ride out their horses all the way to the winning post. Wyatt had, of course, been substituted. This time

Nougat finished two lengths in front of Carlos, with the weights being carried similar to the day before. The fact that they were placed fifth and sixth was irrelevant. The matter was referred to the Stewards of the Jockey Club. They banned Wyatt from riding and training for two years. This tough sentence took into consideration five previous convictions of misconduct. Nougat's owner Jacob Bayliss was a bookmaker, but no charges were made against him.

Wyatt didn't learn his lesson. He was a witness in an 1881 trial at the Old Bailey giving evidence against William Lane, a fraudster who sold tips and claimed to his victim that he was getting inside information from Wyatt, who was riding and training again by now. Wyatt denied having any knowledge of Lane. Quite possibly he was telling the truth then, and that Lane was taking his name in vain, but there is more than a hint of no smoke without fire about Wyatt. In the course of his evidence he stated that he had ridden at every Epsom spring meeting for the last ten years, which wasn't true; he had been banned for part of that time.

Nobody twigged that, but they could hardly fail to notice Wyatt on Brilliancy at Sandown in 1883. The mare was unplaced on the first day of the meeting. On the second she was backed so heavily that bookmakers eventually refused to take any more bets. She won easily. The stewards were on the case immediately. Wyatt and Brilliancy's owner were barred for life from the Turf, the mare was disqualified from all of her winning races, and the owner was ordered to repay all the prize money. Following this decisive blow Wyatt's health declined and he died aged 39 six years later.

Amateur riders were much more prevalent in the late nineteenth and early twentieth centuries, over jumps and on the flat. Many were as good as the professionals, and apart from their weight there were fewer restrictions than nowadays about riding against the pros. One of the best amateurs, and certainly the least savoury, was George Alexander Baird, alias Mr Abington or "The Squire", who inherited a huge sum at an early age. He had a burning desire to win, either riding one of his own large string or on somebody else's. His ruthlessness

The Club Stand, before it was extended (Racing Illustrated/courtesy of Tim Cox)

and combative nature frequently got him into trouble, yet he unquestionably had genuine talent. In May 1888 he was asked to ride the speedy but wayward Bismarck at Windsor. The pair clicked, and the horse broke so fast he galloped to an eight length win, a spectacular display that appeared to herald a change in the horse's attitude. Bismarck was aimed at some lofty prizes. However, in the Stewards Cup, without The Squire on board, he threw a winning chance away by veering in the closing stages. Author George Moore described a very similar incident in his novel Esther Waters, the first part of which is set in a training yard in West Sussex a few miles from the coast, which was where Bismarck had been moved to come under the care of Alfred Day. Baird, weakened by too much of the high life and depressed at his declining ability in the saddle, died at the age of 33.

George Fordham, who rode the inaugural winner at Windsor, rode his last race there on Leopold Rothschild's Aladdin in August 1884. His 2,587 career winners would have been a record if it had not been for the phenomenal Fred Archer, who twice rode four winners in a day at Windsor among his 2,748 career winners. They were condensed into just sixteen years whereas Fordham's spanned 33.

After Archer's suicide in 1886 there were no "household name" jockeys until after the war, when Steve Donoghue and then Gordon Richards came to prominence. Even so, the best flat jockeys, who were mainly based at Newmarket or elsewhere in the south, often rode at Windsor. Punters were well served by Tommy Loates, a three-time champion jockey who in 1894 and 1896 rode five winners in a day at Windsor. On the latter occasion his brother Sam finished runner-up in four of the five races Tommy won. In April 1903 fifteen-year-old Jack Watts rode five winners, but he retired from the saddle relatively young in order to become a trainer.

CHAPTER FIVE – THE NEW JUMPS COURSE

Egham races had struggled on, but in 1881 there were reports of gangs of 25-30 threatening racegoers. The police were unable to cope and announced that they would not attend again after the 1884 races were held. This was a boost for Windsor, whose meetings were much better conducted. The Frails improved security after a riot at Shrewsbury races in 1878.

Futile attempts to keep Egham alive carried on until February 1888, when the management committee decided not to persevere any longer. The portable grandstand and several other temporary buildings assembled for each race meeting were auctioned. The grandstand is believed to have been re-erected at Hawthorn Hill, a little course near Maidenhead which had had its first meeting the year before. It was mainly used for military steeplechases. In the 1920s the Prince of Wales rode there on a few occasions before he became Edward VIII and, after his abdication, Duke of Windsor. It had few fixtures and after the Second World War the course was used for flapping (unrecognised, unlicensed horse racing) and Arab races before eventually being turned into a golf course by Clive Smith, a former pupil of Windsor Grammar School best known for owning the great Kauto Star.

In 1888 the Frail brothers saw an opportunity to get more use from the track and constructed a complete loop from the winning post turning left and running alongside the river to make a figure of 8 track for jump races. This circled the paddock, which was opposite the stands behind the winning post.

The course ran the wrong way (to our eyes) round the far loop. That is to say, that after running right to left along the riverside, where four fences were jumped, the intersection was reached – but instead of going straight on the field would bear right, keeping near the river and heading towards the six furlong start, jumping three more fences. They would then turn left, almost immediately jumping another, and then left again where three more obstacles would be taken near where the marina is today. The far loop was bigger then than it is now. At the intersection they would bear right and meet two more fences before the winning post.

The two mile hurdle races started by the river in the back straight facing towards the town, turned sharp right to come past the winning post, and then took the same line as the flat race course, i.e. running away from the stands to the intersection, bearing left onto the far loop and then right near the six furlong start and finishing in the usual direction.

Once the steeplechase fences were built the new course was first used for a hunt meeting, that of Mr W H Grenfell's Harriers, at the end of April. Mr Grenfell, later Lord Desborough, used his family's wealth to subsidise his career as a public servant by doing a multitude of good works. He was an all-round sportsman too, rowing for Oxford in the boat race, winning a silver medal when representing Britain as a fencer, climbing the Matterhorn and swimming the Niagara Falls rapids. For the Rays Meadow race meeting he offered prizes of between £10 and £80, to be competed for by amateur jockeys. The first event was actually a match, to be run on the flat over two miles. R H Morten's The Druid won by six lengths from Mr H Smith-Turberville's Cover Point. Another of the winners that day was Climb-Axe, bearing his owner Sir Cuthbert Slade to his first victory as a jockey. That pair cleaned up in hunt and military meetings, winning seven races in a row at one stage and 16 out of 30 in all.

It was a useful dry run for a "proper" meeting, but as happened with the Frails' original attempts to start racing at Windsor, the weather intervened and the first National Hunt fixture for professionals was delayed a week because of frost. The two-day meeting got under way in miserably wet conditions on 21 December, and it was beset with problems. A two mile hurdle race for hunters was won by Lord Molynoo, which was followed by an objection that the runners had only jumped seven hurdles instead of eight. It was eventually overruled.

The second race had just two runners and then three went to post for the third race, a two and a half mile chase. The favourite, Louisa, refused at the third fence and after being urged over it continued until falling with a mile to go. Her rider didn't persist any further and this left Gamecock and Chancery to fight out the finish, the latter prevailing by a short head. Louisa's owner then objected that the race had been run over two and three quarter miles instead of the advertised two and a half. One wonders what he would have done if his mare had won. The stewards found that an amateurish mistake had indeed been made and ordered the race to be re-run at the end of the day. Gamecock's connections didn't accept the challenge and Louisa jumped round willingly enough to beat Chancery.

The fourth event was another duel, but not for long as the favourite Sachem refused at the third fence and left Prime Cheddar to finish alone. In the next, four set out but one bolted and two fell, leaving The Sikh to win from one that remounted. The sixth was a two-runner race on the flat, and at the end of it the judge called a dead heat. They ran it again and Brunswick won cosily.

The second day of the meeting had slightly bigger fields and less controversy, although every favourite was beaten. In the finale Gamecock, who won almost 50 races according to his prolific trainer Arthur Yates, got his revenge over Louisa. She reverted to type by falling.

Few courses sought fixtures in December and January. The weather meant gate money would be less than in summer, and the risk of abandonments was much greater. The advantage was that because there were fewer meetings, clashes were not a problem, and it was easier to arrange a postponement for anything up to a week in the hope that the weather improved. The Frails knew the risks and had doubtless worked out that jumping could be profitable. Not until 1895 was the notion of insuring meetings against cancellations explored. Another two-day meeting had been planned for February 1889, the Household Brigade had a day in April and the highlight of a two-day meeting in May was Reliance winning for the Prince of Wales. The owner of the runner-up objected, optimistically and unsuccessfully.

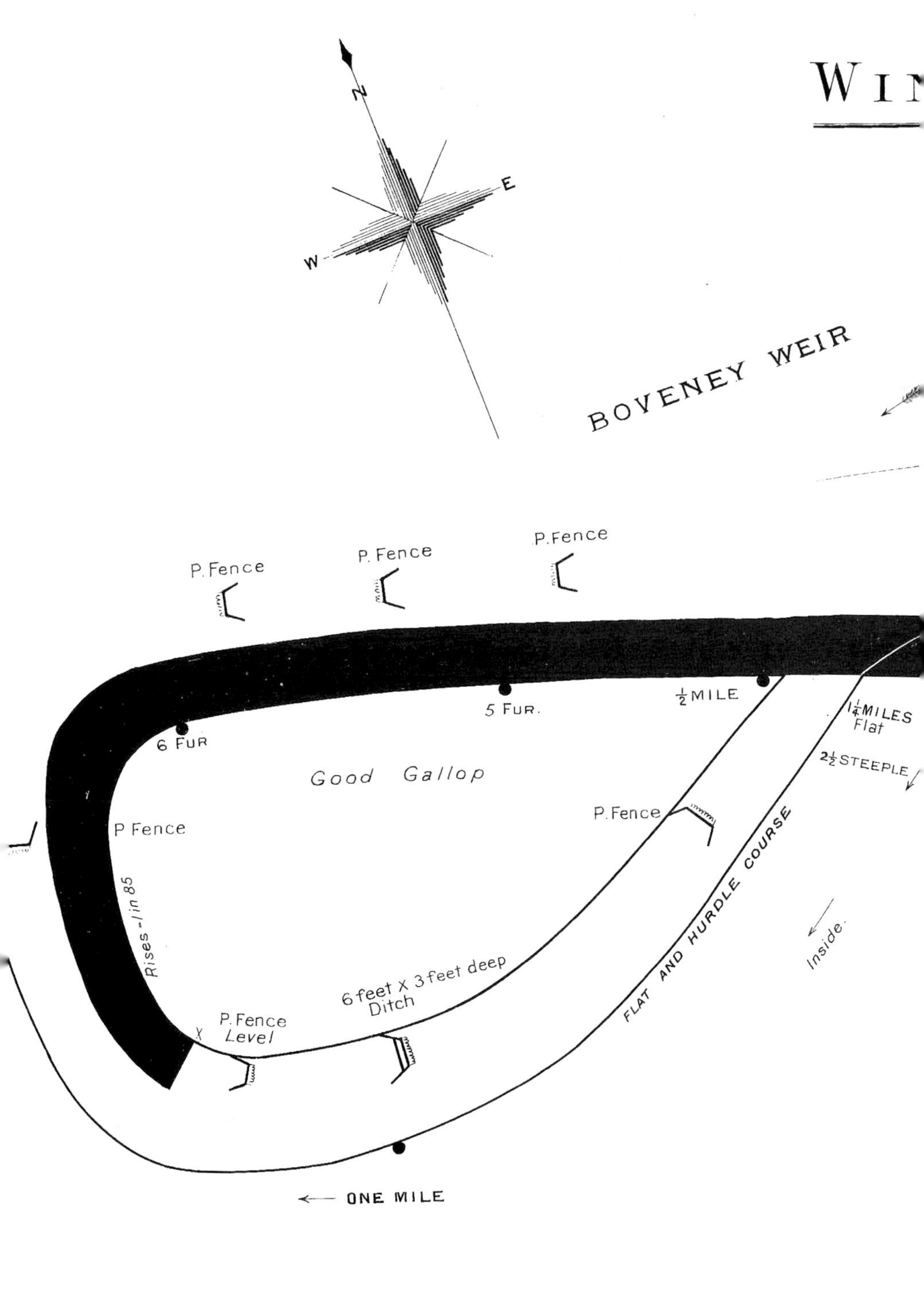

WIN
N
E
W
BOVENEY WEIR
P. Fence
P. Fence
P. Fence
6 FUR
5 FUR.
½ MILE
1¼ MILES
Flat
2½ STEEPLE
Good Gallop
P Fence
P. Fence
Rises -1 in 85
FLAT AND HURDLE COURSE
Inside.
6 feet X 3 feet deep
Ditch
P. Fence
Level
ONE MILE

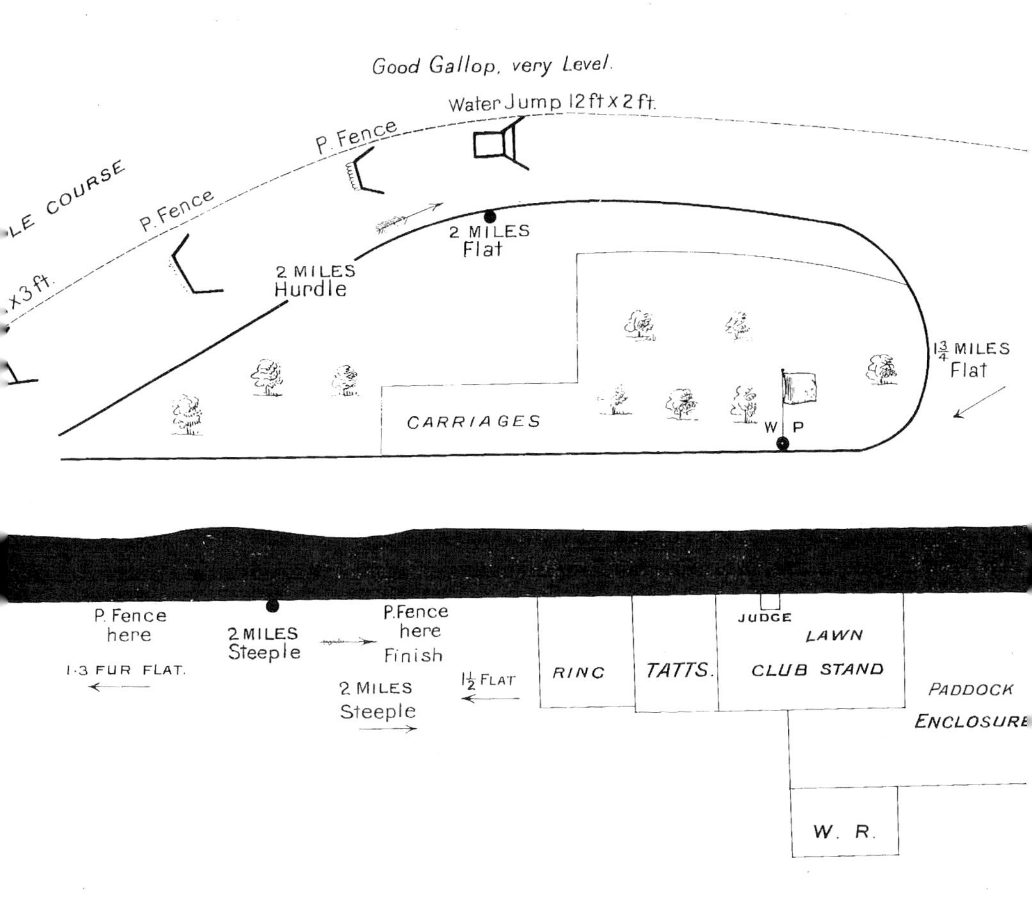

The configuration of the track in 1907; note the direction the jump races were run in

Jumping took root. Harsher training regimes, which were apt to sour horses more, standards of jockeyship, racecourse design, fence building, turf management and the relative cheapness and availability of horses made racing a very different world. By our standards, an intolerably high percentage of fallers was common at most jump meetings. It was accepted then. Horses were still the main form of transport and the sight of one that was being whipped by its driver, lame or dead would not be out of the ordinary. And in the pre-car age horses were plentiful; if one died, it was straightforward enough to get another.

Disastrous train crashes were more frequent;health and safety was unheard of. Two within a year affected Windsor racegoers. A few days before Christmas 1899 twenty policemen who had been doing duty at the races were in a train on the branch line returning to Slough when it collided with the Bristol express. Luckily there were few injuries. Next June there was a much more serious incident at Slough. While a train from Paddington to Windsor, full of racegoers, had halted there an express from London ploughed into the back of it, killing five and injuring 70.

In an 1892 two-horse race at Windsor Gadabout had fallen and repeatedly refused before Sherlock, the jockey, gave up and returned to the paddock. However, the owner, Mr Kennedy, was not satisfied and told his jockey to go back and try again in order to get second place money. By this time the judge had left his box and whatever Gadabout did would not be officially recognised. The stewards told Sherlock not to go out onto the course again, and summoned Kennedy, who refused to go and meet them. Piqued, they reported him to the National Hunt Committee. He turned up to that but declined to apologise to the Windsor stewards for ignoring them, with the result that he was fined £25.

Although the stewards were often appointed on the basis of the old boy network, that didn't automatically mean the quality of their judgement, depth of knowledge and devotion to duty should be denigrated. However, one can question those aspects of the character

Racing in the early 1900s; note the length of the irons (Sporting Sketches/courtesy of Tim Cox)

A close finish in 1902, with the old paddock in the centre of the course (Sporting Sketches/courtesy of Tim Cox)

Today's paddock in 1905 (Sporting Sketches/courtesy of Tim Cox)

of Captain Wiggie Weyland, a steward at a Windsor meeting. There was no sign of him when he was needed to hear an objection, so an official was sent to search for him. The Captain was found among the ranks of bookmakers. He sent a message back to the stewards' room to say he would rejoin them once he'd finished betting on the result of the objection.

In terms of the standard of racing, you were more likely to see a decent horse at a Windsor jump meeting than one on the flat. In those days the Cheltenham Festival did not exist and the Grand National was the be all and end all of the National Hunt season. Windsor attracted National winners and contenders. Gamecock had won the 1887 Grand National. In 1891 Father O'Flynn won a maiden hunters' hurdle en route to six victories elsewhere that year and triumph at Aintree the next. The Midshipmite won 32 races in all, one of his twelve successes in 1892 being a Windsor hurdle. He couldn't ever stay the extreme National distance of four and a half miles, though.

In February of the same year Cloister ran poorly at Windsor but perked up to win a two-horse race there easily prior to finishing runner-up in the National for the second year in a row; he won it by 40 lengths the year after. Cloister was another trained by Arthur Yates, who had a huge number of horses in his Hampshire stable, which benefited courses such as Windsor that were nearby. In the fortnight before the 1894 National Cloister's odds fluctuated from as short as 6/4 to 6/1 and then back down to 2/1. This was after he had been galloped two miles one day, three the next and four and a half two days later! At a Windsor meeting shortly after this his owner Charles Duff found the bookmakers eager to oppose him. One bookie offered him £2,500 to £1,000 as many times as he liked. Duff telegraphed the stable and learned that the vet had found Cloister was slightly lame. How did the bookies at Windsor know before he did? The lameness got worse and the horse was withdrawn from the National a few days later. A similar sequence of events occurred the year after. Duff believed the horse was nobbled. Yates understandably thought otherwise, but the bookmakers' intelligence network was, then as now, a model for MI5.

Duff had the satisfaction of owning two more Grand National winners, by which time he was known as Sir Charles Assheton-Smith.

In January 1896 The Soarer was well backed for a race at Windsor but was beaten by an outsider. Two months later he was a 40/1 shot for the Grand National and won it. His rider, David (later General Sir David) Campbell, was thereafter known as "Soarer" Campbell.

1903 saw the sudden death of John Frail's second son John Ernest, aged 56. The eldest, Charles Simpson, had died four years earlier – which led to the need to put the remaining 19 years of the racecourse lease up for auction, along with the grandstands, the Club Stand, Tattersall's Enclosure and the paddock. The rent was £600 per annum, which was considered cheap in view of the number of race meetings there now. The successful bidder was John Edward Davies, the chairman of the Manchester Race Company, who paid £22,000 for it. He was acting on behalf of Charles Frail junior and Frederick Phillips, the adopted son of John Ernest Frail. This pair created the Windsor Racecourse Company Ltd, whose £30,000 share capital was to be used to acquire and run the racecourse.

In 1905 a new paddock was laid out on the current site. At the time the Daily Mail said it lacked a little shade, but thought that transplanting some trees from the old one would remedy that. The 23 trees circling it now certainly give it shade, and character.

Sir Charles Nugent's curiously named John MP had useful form before injury kept him off the course for the best part of two years. Because of the long absence he was understandably sent off at 100/1 for the Eton Handicap Hurdle at Windsor in January 1906, yet he beat the even money favourite comfortably. It emerged that Sir Charles possessed veterinary skills and had performed operations on the horse with it anaesthetized. Even better performances after that led to John MP starting at 7/2 favourite for the Grand National, a ridiculous price in an era when those were the odds of getting round. He fell at the Canal Turn. Later he was sold to race in the USA.

The presence of a potential wonder horse from New Zealand

called Noctuiform caused unusual interest in September 1906. He was virtually unbeatable in his home country, and had won the Australian Derby in record time. Mindful of the success of Moifaa, another New Zealand-bred, in the 1904 Grand National, James Buchanan (of whisky fame) paid 5,000 guineas for him (about £570,000 in today's money) and brought him over to England. Noctuiform was made favourite for the Cesarewitch, and although he lost his first three races in this country by the time he appeared at Windsor his acclimatisation was thought complete and he was made odds on to open his account. A large, expectant crowd saw him run dismally. He never recaptured his brilliant Antipodean form, despite numerous attempts, often surprisingly well fancied. By December 1908 he had won just one race worth £100 and Buchanan sold him for a tenth of what he had paid for him. His new owner had no joy either, for next month the horse broke a fetlock in a maiden hurdle. Buchanan usually had better luck, notably with the two Derby winners he owned and bred in the 1920s, by which time he had become Lord Woolavington.

In amongst the mediocre types running on the flat at Windsor it was possible for a horse such as Warlingham, trained by Robert Sievier, to have a satisfactorily quiet warm-up down the field before winning the 1912 Cesarewitch at 33/1. Sievier habitually won and lost fortunes. His greatest feat was to train Sceptre to win four of the five classics in 1902. His rumoured winnings of £66,000 (£6.7 million today) on Warlingham funded his purchase of the Fitzroy House stables at Newmarket, currently occupied by Michael Bell.

Lord Derby's Light Brigade was a conspicuous exception; this useful three-year-old won his eleventh race of the 1913 season at Windsor in the autumn, scaring away all but one opponent. That little race helped account in a small way for his 10,000 guineas sale to stand as a stallion in the USA.

In May 1914 a new Club stand was opened, the one still in use today. Though it looks at first sight similar to the building in the photographs dating from the turn of the century, it is definitely longer. It is not certain whether the original was extended or replaced with a wholly new structure. What is clear is that it met with general approbation at the time. "In place of the old stand a most imposing structure now adorns the racecourse. It will hold some 800 people, and a marked feature is that there are tip up seats, from which in wet weather a view of the racing can be had all the way round. There is also a nice tea lounge at the back, and everyone spoke in praise of what had been accomplished." This is still in place today, with the indoor panelling evoking a bygone era when everyone knew their place and the sun never set on the British Empire.

CHAPTER SIX
RACING IN THE FIRST WAR

The assassination of the heir to the Austro-Hungarian Empire in the Balkans in June 1914 was the catalyst for a chain of events that led to Britain declaring war on Germany in August. Racing was halted for three weeks and then resumed, much as before except that racecards, such as those at Windsor's September meeting, carried a full page advertisement saying, "Your King & Country Need You. In the great national emergency that now confronts the Empire, additional men are urgently needed for His Majesty's Regular Army." There were age, height, chest measurement and fitness requirements, and details of how to join. At the bottom of the page was "God Save The King." It was thought the war wouldn't last long, and Windsor staged meetings through the winter.

As time went by the morality of the continuation of horse racing was debated; was it right to continue such a frivolous pursuit while thousands of men were giving their lives in battle? Wouldn't resources be better spent on the war effort? Or should racing continue, to show that we were not allowing the Kaiser to upset our normal daily activities? And to give our servicemen when they were on leave, and indeed the rest of the population, some amusement during such troubled times?

Men in khaki accounted for a third of the crowd at Windsor on 22 May 1915, three days after the government had announced that racing was about to be suspended everywhere apart from a few meetings at Newmarket. After the last race the crowd sang the National Anthem with gusto, and followed with three cheers for the King and Queen. They couldn't really believe this was the last racing for the foreseeable future. There was a feeling that further talks would soon restore fixtures to some tracks where there would be no disruption to local factories producing munitions or military equipment. The authorities, however, feared absenteeism more than real physical danger. No special trains to the races were permitted. Later in the war admission prices were raised considerably, partly due to the imposition of an Entertainments Tax, a further obstacle to the ordinary man in the street attending, even if he had time to go racing.

Jump racing resumed in the winter of 1915/16 at Windsor, Lingfield, Hawthorn Hill, and at Colwall Park in Herefordshire. John Saville, in his excellent book about wartime racing Insane and Unseemly, relates that the National Hunt Committee was able to swing this by emphasising to the Board of Trade the smallness and insignificance of these meetings. Northern owners, trainers, and jockeys had to do without. Windsor had two-day meetings in January and February 1916 that featured previous Grand National winners Covertcoat and Ally Sloper, and in March, the latter being subject to a week's postponement due to flooding. The water hadn't entirely receded when the race meeting took place – horses were saddled on the inside of the course where the old paddock was, as the new one was now a lake.

It involved Berkshire hosting two valuable races transferred from Manchester, the Jubilee Hurdle and the Lancashire Chase. The latter hadn't been far behind the Grand National in terms of importance and in some years its prize money of up to £2,000 exceeded that of the Aintree event. The Windsor version was only worth £300 and it resulted in a win for Templedowney, who overcame a poor display at Lingfield a fortnight earlier to beat the 1915 winner, Vermouth by ten lengths. A French chaser, Clitias, who had once finished second in the Grand Steeplechase de Paris (worth a staggering £8,000), perplexed his owner by running a stinker, although taking a fortnight to get from France to Epsom must have been a factor. A week later Vermouth got his revenge in the specially-arranged Racecourse Association Steeplechase at Gatwick, the alias for a substitute Grand National; Aintree was also shut down.

Quite apart from the moral issue of whether racing should continue, competing and at times contradictory views of different parts of the government meant that racing during the war was very much a stop-go affair. Flat racing was only permitted at Newmarket in 1916 until July, when Windsor was one of a few southern courses allocated some fixtures. Unprecedentedly, a £1,000 prize was put up for the St George's Handicap. This was won by Lord Derby's good sprinter Phalaris, who in the course of his career was victorious in 16 of his 24 races and became a successful stallion. As it turned out, an even brighter star was on display that day. Diadem brushed aside three moderate opponents in a two-year-old race. She was to win the following year's 1,000 Guineas and become a top sprinter, winning 24 races out of 39 in a career that spanned six years. The Diadem Stakes run on Champions Day at Ascot is named after her.

Despite the need for horses at the front line, which had meant some thoroughbreds being requisitioned by the authorities, enough had slipped through the net to keep racing going. December 1916's meeting had healthy fields of 27, 19, 12, 14, 21 and 3 on the first day; 11, 12, 12, 24, 14 and 19 on the next. Weather permitting, racing carried on through the first quarter of 1917. Again Gatwick staged the War National, preceded by the Lancashire Chase at Windsor, in which Captain Dreyfus beat Templedowney, with the winners of four past and future Nationals (Ballymacad, Ally Sloper and Poethlyn twice) unplaced. Thanks to the war, the standard of jump racing at Windsor was higher than it had ever been.

As happened the previous spring, the mood swung back against racing, fuelled by complaints about hundreds of cars seen going to the races despite the petrol shortage. The War Cabinet made clear their view that racing should stop in May. By the end of July the pendulum had swung the other way and Windsor was allowed three Saturdays for flat racing in what was left of the summer, with Brighton, Manchester, Ayr and Stockton also being allowed to race.

A limited programme of National Hunt racing in the winter of 1917/18 was curtailed further by the weather. Frost and snow caused the postponement of Windsor's January meeting for a week. February's was almost entirely lost to fog. The Lancashire Chase and the Jubilee Hurdle went back to Manchester. More courses were given flat fixtures for 1918, and Windsor managed one such day in April before it was, yet again, suspended everywhere except Newmarket as a result of bad news from the front. With no end to the war in sight, next month came the announcement there would be no jump racing at all next winter.

Happily the late summer and autumn of 1918 brought a rapid change in the Allies' fortunes and the war came to end on 11 November. Restrictions on racing were promptly lifted, but logistically it was impossible to arrange meetings anywhere in what was left of that year. Windsor was quick off the mark in 1919 but once again the weather interfered. They raced on 31 January, where the field sizes were 3, 1, 3, 1, 4 and 4, only for the following day to be abandoned because of snow. February's meeting was called off because of flooding.

Post-war euphoria meant crowds flocked to racecourses in huge numbers. Saturday afternoon meetings were described as "inconveniently popular". At Windsor in the summer of 1919 so many were packing into the cheap stand in the Silver Ring it was deemed unsafe. A new larger concrete edifice replaced it.

Gangsters who had been called up during the war, or kept off the racecourse because of the limited opportunities, or simply laid low, returned in force. It was boom time for pickpockets, welshers, protection racketeers and every other type of criminal with an eye to the main chance. A bookmaker's clerk was arrested with 160 counterfeit florins (two-shilling coins) on him. He told the police he had bought them at Windsor races; they could easily be passed into general circulation at a racecourse.

A man who had won £350 at the races was walking back to the station via the riverside, with his hands and a wad of bank notes thrust well down into his trouser pockets. But villains had targeted him and didn't know or didn't care that he was a prominent heavyweight boxer – they outnumbered him and had the element of surprise. Coming up behind him, one pulled his hat down over his eyes, another jabbed his backside with a lady's hatpin. As he put up his fists and prepared to fight, others snatched at the notes in his unguarded pockets and dashed off.

Windsor racegoers could meet additional hazards if travelling by ferry, where on a crowded boat ordinary pickpockets could find easy prey there, especially when deliberately bumping into someone getting on or off. Their more violent counterparts threw passengers into the river if they refused to hand over their wallets. Many buttoned up their pockets and jumped overboard to save their money.

It was widely believed that some of the police and gatemen racecourses employed turned a blind eye, via threats or being paid off. But with the best will in the world, the sheer size of the crowds could make it difficult to catch anyone red-handed or to find alleged miscreants. In addition to various bogus charges that gangs extorted from bookmakers in order to enjoy their "protection", racecourse staff were also suspected of demanding money from them to allow them to bet. There is no reason why Windsor should have been immune from all this skulduggery.

Not until Sir Samuel Scott became Senior Steward of the Jockey Club in 1922 did the rulers of racing begin to acknowledge this lawlessness was their problem. He began a process that would crack down on racecourse gangs, setting up the Jockey Club's own internal police force. Tellingly some of the racecourses were very much against this, and it wasn't until 1925 that a corps of ex-policemen and army officers were in place.

One gang had been defrauding bookies with forged tickets, stealing from their satchels, stealing betting tickets from careless punters and pickpocketing. Suspicion fell on a man dressed as an Army lieutenant after £25 was taken from a bookie's satchel at Windsor races. The ringleader then resorted to mufti but eventually 13 of his gang were arrested at Windsor, and all were convicted.

Order was restored, villains were caught and prosecuted and gang warfare began to diminish. Graham Greene's description of gang warfare in Brighton Rock (1938) was about ten years out of date, but he exploited one high-profile climactic fight at Lewes races that hit the headlines in 1936. Police had been tipped off and were present in sufficient numbers to arrest the protagonists there. Stiff prison sentences were imposed on them.

William Bebbington, one of the leading lights in the new Jockey Club squad, told a tale about a pickpocket he nabbed at Windsor races who pleaded not guilty and hired a well-known barrister to defend himself. One argument he used was that it was impossible for someone not to realise that his pocket was being picked. Sitting next to him while he defended his client was the chief constable, who surreptitiously extracted something from the barrister's pocket. When he finished his speech Bebbington was allowed to ask him a question. "Have you, Mr H, during the time you've been addressing the magistrates, lost anything from your own person?" The barrister was flabbergasted to find his silver cigarette case missing. His client was found guilty, whereupon the court was told about his 19 previous convictions.

The course was used by a film company in 1920 to re-enact a nineteenth century Epsom Derby for a film called The Game of Life. This wasn't the first time the course had been seen on the big screen; a 1915 newsreel shows action from a steeplechase. On the British Film Institute's website Windsor racecourse can be glimpsed a few times in a short science-fiction fantasy from 1924, The Fugitive Futurist. One meeting in 1931 featured Kissing Cup's Race, promoting a film with a racing theme. It was based on the poem of that name which had been shot at the racecourse the year before. This was the third time the now-forgotten poem had been the subject of a film. Since then the racecourse has featured on TV and in films many times, one of the most recent being Suffragette, released in October 2015. The scene where Emily Davison threw herself in the path of the King's horse in the 1913 Derby was filmed eighteen months earlier at Windsor in preference to Tattenham Corner. The Club stand provided an authentic period backdrop to some of the action.

In 1922 the "very able and energetic" management introduced a rule of making all runners carry number cloths, so that racegoers could identify the horses before jockeys mounted. They also had the entire course railed. Things we take for granted today!

Contrary to their normal image, one of the tipsters that frequented the course was a cheerful, good-looking young man who wore a beret. He was popular with the female racegoers, and athletic; in the jumps season he would go out onto the track to help catch loose horses and given half a chance he would ride one back to the unsaddling area.

It became more fashionable to object in National Hunt races between the wars, but it didn't always work to the benefit of the complainant. Bryan Bletsoe, riding the fast-finishing runner-up Amnesty, objected to the winner The Saint IV. There was no apparent reason for it as The Saint IV had been clear of his opponent. The stewards not only dismissed Bletsoe's case, but warned him that his riding was open to suspicion. And a Mr Knight asked for the Windsor stewards to hold an enquiry into the running of his own mare, Lovely Bird, who had been well backed at Gatwick but finished unplaced prior to winning that afternoon. The horse's jockey at Gatwick was cleared of any misdeeds.

The Wisp was disqualified after passing the post first following an objection that he wasn't a maiden when entries for the race closed. This sort of technical objection was very common in the nineteenth century. One imagines that the fault was often noticed by rivals before the race but kept quiet until afterwards, with bets or riding instructions adjusted accordingly. The Wisp's owner was fined 20 guineas for gross carelessness. He was entitled to feel a little hard done by, as other officials also failed to notice the infringement.

Stewards were busy handing out cautions to jockeys – sometimes they were "severely cautioned" – but this had no practical effect. Considering the high number of fallers that occurred at Windsor, the prospect of riding badly trained horses and having to steer clear of those ridden by others, being ticked off at a stewards' enquiry was a minor annoyance for jockeys. Two out of seven finished in one Carry On Steeplechase that didn't live up to its name. Nine fell out of 15 runners in one Over The Top Steeplechase that did. Ten fell and one refused in another chase with 15 runners. There were clues in some

The triple dead heat (Mirrorpix)

horses' names, such as Escaped Lunatic (of whom the form book says with a certain logic "pedigree unknown"), whose owner-rider put up half a stone overweight when falling on the first day of one meeting and pulling up on the second.

History was made at Windsor on 21 September 1923. Fourteen ran in the mile and a quarter Royal Borough Handicap for three-year-olds. As they approached the two furlong pole, the second favourite Dumas was going well and took the lead. The top weight Marvex came with a good late run and then Dinkie came up fastest of all. The three flashed past the post together. The judge – well before the days of the photo-finish camera – could not split them. He called a triple dead heat, a very rare but not unknown occurrence. The most recent had been one at Sandown in 1915 where, incredibly, Dumas's jockey rode one of the three horses concerned. Bookmakers weren't terribly happy at having to do the extra mathematics and pay out on three horses, based on a third of the stake on each. It could have been worse; an 1855 race at Newmarket resulted in a dead heat between four of the five runners. The uniqueness of the Windsor race was due to the fact that a press photographer close to the winning post took a picture of the trio as they passed it. We thereby have proof that the judge's decision was a reasonable one.

In a little race in August 1926 Indiscretion had beaten Capricious. An obvious forecast for a fun bet, but forecast bets weren't taken by the racecourse bookmakers unless there were very few runners and there was no such thing as the Tote … yet.

CHAPTER SEVEN
THE BOOKMAKERS' STRIKE

The laws on betting were confused, and had been for over seventy years. Basically in 1926 one could bet with a credit account by telephone or telegraph, or with cash on the racecourse, but cash betting anywhere else was illegal. The wealthy, apt to bet on credit in large quantities, were treated as though they could manage their betting responsibly, whereas the poor had to be protected from themselves, even if they could only afford a few pennies or shillings here and there. This didn't stop millions of ordinary people betting via a bookie's runner, who would convey cash to and from the local undercover betting office. Licensed betting shops that could operate openly on the high street were decades away.

In order to balance the country's books, the notion of a betting tax appealed not only because it would raise money, but also because of the moral dimension. The latter concerned society's spiritual guardians, the Reverend F A Iremonger being one of them. At the London Diocesan Conference of June 1926 he bemoaned the notion of a betting tax. He said he spoke as someone who knew about racing and he had an account with a bookmaker, as he imaginatively described his uncollected winnings from a five shilling bet at Windsor some 30 years ago. Many saw betting as a vice, and as it was illegal if you were too poor to have a credit account or to go racing, it was akin to taxing something you really shouldn't be doing anyway.

Research on behalf of the Treasury suggested that a tax would reduce the amount of betting turnover by 30%, but the tax charged on that lower level of activity was still worth having. The tax itself was supposed to be 5% on stakes, so anybody wanting a £1 bet was supposed to pay that plus a shilling (5p) to the bookmaker. Winston Churchill, the Chancellor of the Exchequer at the time, had his doubts but was persuaded to go through with the necessary legislation. The tax came into effect on 1 November 1926, the start of a two-day meeting at Birmingham and one at Wye in Kent. Though theoretically it was a tax on all bets, in practice bookmakers made deductions of 6d in the £ (2.5%) from winning bets. Turnover was significantly down.

Before racing at Windsor on 3 November a group of bookmakers decided not to chalk up any prices, in protest against the tax. A number of them were against the tax, but didn't want to strike. They were in an awkward position, as life could be made very difficult for them if they defied the others – and the band of heavies recruited to act as pickets. Bemused punters in Tattersalls looked on helplessly, and everyone watched the first race in silence. The same absence of odds offered for the second race was broken when one brave soul called out "6/4 the field". Immediately a swarm of hostile pickets surrounded his joint and he was compelled to toe the line. The horse that would have been that 6/4 favourite, Bohemia, won. A disaffected punter shouted something in favour of the Tote, He too was threatened and police had to intervene. Though there was some betting in the Silver Ring, no starting prices were returned, preventing any off-course credit betting business. The protesting bookmakers agreed to repeat the strike on the second day of the meeting. Agitation of this sort was in vogue; the General Strike was, after all, fresh in people's minds.

Legitimate bookmakers felt aggrieved not only for the administrative inconvenience, expense, and likely loss of business, but also because illegal and back-street bookies would by definition avoid the tax. Indeed, they would prosper as more punters turned to them. Some of the legal bookmakers later resorted to hedging their bets with the illegals – an early form of money laundering. Those who gave credit had to be particularly careful how they selected their clientele, for gambling debts were not recoverable by law.

On the second day of the Windsor meeting pickets were present at Paddington station. 30 or 40 more waited outside the racecourse entrance, professing to be peaceful protesters asking bookmakers not to bet and punters not to go in or not to bet. There were ugly moments when some arriving bookmakers objected to the picketers wearing trademark red rosettes, despite not being in the business themselves. "After heated declaration and some very impolite debate", as the Guardian put it, the rosettes were discarded and the bookmakers went in. The moderates among them stated that their strike the day before was only ever meant to be for that one day.

Inside, Tattersalls was bereft of bookmakers offering odds – not that there were many punters, for The Times reported that only four people paid to go in, knowing the likelihood of being unable to bet. Half a dozen bookmakers traded quietly on the first race in the Silver Ring, where the attendance was healthier. Word got round and the pickets came to remonstrate with them. Reluctantly the bookmakers began to pack up, but then Bebbington arrived and warned the strikers and their pickets in no uncertain terms. Faced with the prospect of being arrested for threatening behaviour, they backed off. Betting resumed, at first tentatively, and then with a little more confidence as it became apparent that Bebbington's words had done the trick.

A red herring to the effect that the trouble was caused by professional punters refusing to bet because of the tax, and thereby prompting bookmakers not to trade, can be dismissed. Rumours of a strike had been circulating weeks prior to the imposition of the tax.

At Newport racecourse that day there was no striking or picketing, but Windsor lost about £2,000 in admissions because of the unavailability of betting or the distaste for being picketed. The attendance at Newbury, racing soon after, suffered because of that fear. Bookmakers traded normally there, as the most vigorous "antis" had decided not to try and continue striking. They had bills to pay, and striking deprived them of their livelihood. And they must have realised that the bigger threat of the Tote might do them even more damage.

The government took an unsympathetic view of the strike and rather than weaken its stance on the tax it strengthened the mood to implement a totalisator, an idea first mooted years before. They had been in use abroad in the nineteenth century but were illegal in Britain. The Tote would not go on strike, would unerringly collect any tax due, and profits could be recycled to the benefit of racing. Its creation was a foregone conclusion after the shenanigans at Windsor. Indeed, the prospect of a Tote monopoly, excluding bookmakers from racecourses, was considered. One can look back on this and regard it as a great chance missed, an opportunity to have guaranteed racing's financial health permanently.

The amount collected from the betting tax was much less than forecast, and the trouble it caused the government led to it being watered down and abolished in 1929, the year that the Tote started operating.

***

The 1920s National winners Sergeant Murphy, Shaun Spadah, Jack Horner and Sprig ran at Windsor before or after their Aintree triumphs. In March 1928 the second running of the Champion Hurdle at Cheltenham was won by Brown Jack. He showed such good form over the sticks, where his form figures were 00311111-0121, that connections decided to try racing him on the flat, aiming at the two mile Ascot Stakes at the Royal meeting. His second ever run on the flat was in the White Lodge Stakes at Windsor in May. This was his first win on the level; it was only by a head, but his battling qualities enabled him to gain the day. Next month he duly won the Ascot Stakes. In all he won 25 races, including Royal Ascot victories seven years in a row, six of them being the two and three quarter mile Queen Alexandra Stakes, the longest flat race in the calendar. While assembling this tremendous sequence Brown Jack became a household name, as he developed a great partnership with his similarly popular jockey Steve Donoghue. Retired immediately after his record-breaking sixth win in the race, Brown Jack's biography was written straight away, a locomotive was named after him and Sir Alfred Munnings made a statue of him to be erected at Ascot.

Windsor had a desperate run of luck with its jumping fixtures, with none taking place between December 1928 and February 1930 due to floods and frost. The new sport of greyhound racing affected the size of the crowds in the cheap enclosures. The Staines dog track near Wraysbury opened in January 1928 and the novelty value brought in good crowds to begin with. The greyhound stadium was soon being used for speedway as well. It closed in 1960.

A horse called Windsor Lad won the Derby and St Leger in 1934 and was a topical choice for the name of the new pub in the Maidenhead Road built soon afterwards. Windsor Lad won ten of his thirteen races, but none were at Windsor. Why was he so named? Perhaps it was to do with the sire of his dam, By George! – George V being the reigning monarch, and a friend of the horse's owner, the Maharaja of Rajpipla. It's more likely the name was a reference to the Maharaja himself, who owned The Manor, a large house in Old Windsor. During the war he donated three Spitfires to the RAF, one of which was named Windsor Lad. When the state of Rajpipla was subsumed into the new independent nation of India the Maharaja opted to retire to The Manor, where he died in 1951.

The future National winner Royal Mail won a little race for amateur riders at Windsor in December 1935. His owner, Mr Thomas, had come over from Paris to ride. Hopefully the value to the race to the winning owner, £82, covered his expenses. A four mile race, the Fringford Chase, was run during the 1930s to serve as a Grand National trial. When Blue Shirt won the 1938 renewal it was his third consecutive win in a four-mile race, a feat it would be almost impossible to achieve nowadays.

The second half of the 1930s was a grim period in the racecourse's history. In September 1937 a bookmaker shot himself during a race meeting. 64 year old Frank Homer hadn't been content with laying horses, which had given him a good living. He tried to become a punter, and lost a lot of money. His brother had had to help him financially more than once but nobody had expected him to commit suicide. After the 3.30 race a policeman noticed Homer walking away from the crowd into a quiet area among some trees, where he produced a gun and fired a single shot.

In November 1938 a 21 year old jockey, Arthur Sharples, was killed while riding La Blottiere during a six furlong race with 35 runners. With a furlong to go Prelude, ridden by Sharples's friend Albert Taylor, was cannoned into by another horse, bringing him down and causing La Blottiere to fall as well. Nothing was found amiss with the track before racing or after the fatality and there was no suggestion of foul riding. Safety standards were minimal in comparison with today, and blame was rarely apportioned where there were falls causing injury to horse or jockey. Such was the case here, even though it should have been obvious that such a huge field of sprinters was asking for trouble. The coroner recorded a verdict of accidental death. Taylor suffered concussion and bruises, and the shock of Sharples's death made him consider giving up riding.

35 wasn't a course record, for 42 faced the starter in a race in 1935. And when 30 lined up for a two mile hurdle, the starter needed to arrange them in two rows. It's not known whether he asked for triers to go in front, non-triers in the rear, but the winner did come from the front row. At least one two mile maiden chase started with 25 runners, with the first fence having room for only about eight abreast.

This period also saw the deaths of Charles Simpson Frail's sons, Charles and Cecil, both of whom were involved with the management of Windsor and other courses. Cecil was particularly associated with Haydock, where a race was named after him. Charles was chairman of the Windsor racecourse company and its manager up to the time of his death. He had lived in Windsor for years, some of that time in the Mill House at Clewer. Approaching 70 years of age and facing retirement was Frederick Phillips, at various times Clerk of the Course and auctioneer. He, the adopted son of John Ernest Frail, was the last of the Frails to be involved with the running of the course.

CHAPTER EIGHT
RACING IN THE SECOND WAR

With the demise of the Frails the chairmanship passed to a younger man, Henry Arthur Steel, a local businessman and sports enthusiast. After training as an architect he branched out into property development. He played a major part in the building of South Ruislip as suburbia extended further north and west of London between the wars. His involvement with the racecourse began in the 1920s, and it became a major interest for his family. His young daughter Bindi used to collect flowers from neighbours' gardens to make the racecourse look prettier. She and a friend used to go to Newbury races with her father and they were left to their own devices with ten shillings each to amuse themselves. The only proviso was that they were not to bet in the last race, so that they could get away quickly.

Steel had horses in training at Epsom with Peter Thrale. His best was the high-class chaser Macaulay. This horse won several races and his performance at Sandown in January 1939 marked him as extra special. Carrying 12 stone 7 pounds in the three mile five furlong Prince's Steeplechase, he was a hundred yards behind the leader coming to the third last fence, when suddenly he started making up ground hand over fist. Jumping the last full of running, he won by six lengths in a time eight seconds faster than that clocked a year ago by the five-time Cheltenham Gold Cup winner Golden Miller. The handicapper reacted by allocating Macaulay 12 stone 4 pounds for the Grand National. In all probability he would have been aimed at the Gold Cup if he hadn't broken down at Hurst Park in his next race. He was very difficult to keep sound after that and didn't win again.

John Knight, who had moved down from Lancashire in 1937, was the company secretary and racecourse manager. He trained as an accountant and had worked at the Manchester track, restoring it to profitability and putting it back on its feet. Windsor had similar financial problems in the mid-30s and he was asked by the Frails to sort them out. Things didn't go well to begin with. A 2/6 charge for parking was introduced for each car not being used by an owner, trainer or annual member. Those individuals were meant to pay to enter the car park and claim the money back from the racecourse office. This bureaucracy caused uproar, and assurances were given that the experiment would not be repeated. The same day the Boveney Hurdle, over a mile and a half, ended in controversy when the riders of the two leaders made no attempt to ride a finish. It was so blatant it was clear that both jockeys believed they had another circuit to go. There was a neck between them as they passed the winning post. Fortunately both were 100/8 shots; if a well-fancied horse had finished second, the mood of the crowd might not have been as jocular.

That wasn't Knight's fault, but he suffered further embarrassment on the day it was realised the weighing room clock was fast. Several races were started a minute early, and credit bookmakers had to refuse bets telegraphed to them before the advertised start time but after the races were under way. The refundable car park charges were, contrary to previous expectations, persisted with. There were rumblings about the state of the stands, which were considered inadequate for the big crowds that continued to throng the flat meetings, and the "fairy bridge", the narrow little bridge over the Mill Stream that was the only way in and out of the course for motorists. Trying to get away at the end of a summer Saturday afternoon could take hours.

From 1937 there was a steady stream of disagreements reported in The Times about the judge's verdict when there were close finishes. One of the first and most flagrant cases was when a grey called Satyr was the only challenger in the last two furlongs to the winner Rusky. The Times's correspondent was sure Satyr had been beaten less than a length. Yet the judge declared Sequalo was second, and Satyr fourth. Sequalo was down the field according to the journalist, and to his jockey, who did not ride back to the unsaddling enclosure for the winner and placed horses. Later that year Archman was declared the runner-up when he had in fact fallen at the second last fence. That was soon corrected.

Until now the judge had been positioned on the stands side, but in the spring of 1938 a new elevated box for him was built on the inside of the track. Giving height was a good move in theory, yet the debatable verdicts increased. In August Mickey Mouse appeared to have beaten Lost Scent very narrowly, with Golden Martlet was a fast-finishing third just a neck away. The judge, however, made it a dead heat between the first two, with the third a length away. Later that day everyone except him thought Leading Topic had beaten Invisible by a neck. His decision was greeted with a brief stunned silence before a chorus of jeers. At the September meeting there were short heads between the first three in the opening race, but the one that appeared to have finished fifth was placed third and the one thought to be third was placed fourth. In November onlookers thought Heru had beaten Too Dear by a head, but again the judge believed the contrary. Alastair was placed second in another race where the consensus was that he finished fourth.

At the end of a selling chase in February 1939 racegoers were divided in their opinions about the winner in a close finish, so the judge was probably justified to call a dead heat. In August punters thought Orcades had beaten Sedan by a neck, but the judge's verdict was Sedan by a short head. In December Custom House appeared to beat Psychic Bid by a neck, whereas the judge decided the opposite. On the numberboard the board giving the winning distance as one length was about to be slotted into place, before being hurriedly replaced with one saying the margin was a head.

In June 1940 Sacred Fish won, though many thought Burytown had passed the post in front. Knight of the Garden was beaten at least two lengths into third but judge said a head. Later Gordon Richards thought he had won on Oubliette and as he returned to the enclosures he kept looking in disbelief at the numberboard, as if he was expecting the numbers of the first two to be swapped at any moment.

Charitably, one should say that the judge was in the best place to decide and it was a difficult angle to read – and still is! Malcolm Hancock was usually the man on duty at Windsor. He was an experienced racecourse judge, having started in 1920, following in his father's footsteps. Prior to that he was awarded the Military Cross for carrying a wounded soldier to safety in full view of the enemy at Gallipoli. He was just 18 years old at the time. Soon after he was wounded so badly that he needed six months to recover. During the Second World War Hancock had fewer opportunities to officiate at the racecourse, for he rejoined the Army and rose to the rank of Honorary Major. One of his roles was the organisation of escape routes for the royal family should a German invasion occur.

Roger Mortimer tells a story in his book The Flat that after a particularly loud protest about a photo finish verdict (the camera was introduced at Newmarket in 1947 and spread slowly to other tracks) the official said, "Oh dear, I'm afraid my spectacles may have let me down again… I never really wanted to be a Judge but Weatherbys asked me and I did not like to hurt their feelings by refusing." That wasn't Hancock, who recorded an account of his life for posterity, including a little about his judging career, which can be heard on the Imperial War Museum's website.

The Duke and Duchess of Kent were part of the huge crowd in June 1939 who enjoyed an entertaining auction after the seller for two-year-olds. The bidding started at 50 guineas and the horse was ultimately knocked down for 1,550 to Steve Donoghue, who by now was a trainer. He was bidding on behalf of a Mr Roll, who was so keen to get the horse he nearly topped his trainer's final bid.

It's an ill wind, and one of the perverse consequences of a World War was the spotlight falling on Windsor as it was, again, one of the few courses to host racing. This time it was the quality of flat racing that rose to unprecedented heights.

The moral and political arguments for and against racing were similar to those in the First World War, although transport restrictions that previously reflected the importance of the railway network and the

Henry Steel

comparatively small number of car users were reversed, as petrol was the first thing rationed when war broke out in September 1939. The stop-go attitude resurfaced, veering from the suspension of racing to negotiating and implementing its limited resumption before the prevailing mood darkened and it was wound down again. In this section of the book I have again relied on John Saville's definitive study of racing in the World Wars, Insane and Unseemly.

Kempton had quickly been annexed by the military and their Boxing Day meeting could not take place. That fixture was nowhere near as renowned as it became later. Indeed, the centrepoint today – the King George VI Chase, the mid-season highlight of the National Hunt season – had only been inaugurated in 1937 and was run in February. Windsor stepped in to fill the void. The main event was the Herne The Hunter Chase, the subject of the first BBC broadcast from

Windsor racecourse, with commentary by Raymond Glendenning. The race, a feature of midwinter Windsor cards until 1965, was named after the ghost with antlers on his head who haunts Windsor Forest and is referred to in Shakespeare's The Merry Wives of Windsor. Lord Stalbridge's six-year-old Bogskar won on the second day of the meeting and went on to win the Grand National in the spring of 1940, partnered by RAF Sergeant Mervyn Jones. In between those races a vicious cold spell caused the abandonment of racing for almost two months. At Windsor's March meeting the Cheltenham Gold Cup favourite Roman Hackle enjoyed an easy win over two miles giving weight to his opponents prior to winning the big race over a mile and a quarter further five days later with equal ease.

By May 1940 it was clear that the war was going to last for a long time and all racing was cancelled – only in the next few weeks for it to be allowed to resume in part, then whittled down and finally confined to Newmarket. The next attempt to relax that situation included meetings planned for Windsor in September, but they were called off because of the fear of a Nazi invasion. Hitler tried to impose an air and sea blockade with the aim of making Britain seek peace or surrender. The RAF fought the Luftwaffe for command of the skies over London and the south east and after a desperate struggle gained victory by the end of October. The invasion was averted, at least for the time being. By then the Blitz had begun, and in the next three months 30,000 bombs were dropped on London. It continued until May 1941, but failed to disrupt factories and ports significantly. Moreover, the civilian population remained resolutely cheerful and unbowed. Despite the risk of one's home or workplace being blown to bits and the deprivations of rationing, life went on as normally as possible under the circumstances.

Once the Americans had joined the war in December 1941 and the Eastern Front was tying up more of Hitler's resources, a relaxation of restrictions to the racing programme was permitted in 1942. Windsor was given a couple of fixtures to start with, on Whit Saturday and Monday. The first meeting there for two years drew 10,000 people, despite travel restrictions. Not only was petrol rationed, but trainers were restricted in terms of the distance they could travel to race meetings. Here and at other wartime meetings motorists were apt to be quizzed by government officials to check that they had legitimate business to drive to the races. Young men and women in civilian garb were challenged by a combination of ordinary and military police and if they didn't have proof of identity they were taken for further questioning to the racecourse police station; every course had one on race days. Hundreds arrived on rowing boats.

Pedestrians coming from the town would turn right at Mill Lane a quarter of a mile before the modern-day racecourse entrance. The flats on the right, Villiers Court, used to be the Duke of Edinburgh public house. Along the first part of this road are some handsome Victorian buildings, one with a plaque dating from 1869; the fourth on the left is the Swan public house, closed and up for sale at the time of writing. Coaches used to line up on the left hand side of the road. Clewer Cottage, on the right, used to be the village shop.

After the Victorian houses on the left of Mill Lane end there are modern houses, but up to the late 1950s a brick wall extended all the way to the Mill House at the end of the road. Gates gave entry to the Clewer Park estate, a playground for the local youngsters.

On the right of Mill Lane, The Stables used to be riding stables, but they weren't connected with the racecourse. The older house on the corner of Clewer Court Road has a blue plaque marking it as the home of Mariquita Tennant, a Spanish lady who was active in rescuing the fallen women of Windsor in the 1840s. Turn right there and once past the last Victorian house, modern houses occupy the site of the old stables for the racecourse and the Royal Windsor Horse Show. They extended up to where the dual carriageway runs. Horse boxes used to park next to them in Stovell Road, which was parallel to today's road of the same name. No trace of the racecourse stables remain.

On the other side of Clewer Court Road is St Andrew's Church, reputedly the site of a place of worship for a thousand years. The graveyard contains the remains of Owen Allum, a 17 year old Windsor telegraph boy, one of the few bodies recovered from the Titanic disaster. He was going to live with his father in the USA.

Horses, once saddled, were led from the stables past the churchyard back to Mill Lane, where they turned right to go up to the Mill House. This is now a dead end, but there used to be a path through to the racecourse for them, which pedestrians had to pay a toll to use.

Windsor acquired five more dates later as Salisbury, where most of the southern flat meetings were originally allocated, became unavailable. Entries could only be accepted from stables south of the Trent, which accounts for the success of Epsom trainers in five races out of six at one meeting. Large or very large attendances were reported every time. The King's two-year-old filly Sunblind was a popular winner in October, though she wasn't in the same league as her owner's Sun Chariot, who won the Triple Crown that year.

In 1943 Windsor was awarded five days from April onward and the road travel limits were extended, so more trainers could send horses there. A 3pm start to the 10 April meeting gave factory workers extra time to get to the track after their Saturday morning shifts ended. 138 cars and 59 taxis were logged bringing people to the racecourse. In the House of Commons the Minister of Fuel was asked for his observations. He stated that this use of petrol was for legitimate business purposes and he observed that "a certain amount of relaxation must be had by the people."

Military uniforms were present in great numbers, with Americans swelling the crowds too. Mayhem ensued on Easter Monday, 26 April, as there was a bus workers' strike and police decided to stop every driver coming into Windsor to check their papers. That didn't prevent another huge crowd (30,000 according to one estimate) from attending and seeing one of the track's best ever days of flat racing, with a number of Classic hopefuls on display. Tommy Carey rode five winners, one of them being Dorothy Paget's Straight Deal, who had won impressively over the course last year and finished second in the Dewhurst Stakes. It looked like he was a good horse without being outstanding. He disappointed in the 2,000 Guineas, his next outing after Windsor, before exceeding expectations by winning the Derby, which in wartime was run on the July course at Newmarket.

Miss Paget was a fantastically wealthy eccentric heiress. On one occasion her Rolls Royce broke down on the way to the races. After that she required two cars to take her and her entourage, one following the other in case of another breakdown. During the war she was obliged to make a journey by train and she asked the railway authorities for a carriage to be reserved for herself because she could not bear to sit next to a male stranger; it would make her vomit.

She loved horses infinitely more than men. She chopped and changed trainers and jockeys ruthlessly. Few who gave candid opinions about her lesser lights remained in her employment, or favour. She bet heavily and indiscriminately on her own horses, once with bizarre effect on the Derby betting. Her colt Tuppence, who had cost 6,000 guineas (£400,000 today), was entered for the Derby despite showing very little ability. Her bets at 100/1 brought the price down to 50s and 33s, whereupon misguided rumours of a great gamble snowballed in the last few days leading up to the race, fuelled by housewives putting their tuppences and sixpences on because of its name. Its odds tumbled to the utterly illogical level of 10/1, but it ran like the 100/1 shot it really was to finish nineteenth.

Happily for Windsor, Miss Paget regarded it and Folkestone as her lucky courses, perhaps because her horses usually outclassed most of the opposition; they went off at short prices (helped by her huge bets) and tended to win. 30 of her 40 National Hunt winners there from 1945 onward were favourites, most trained by Fulke Walwyn. She was a frequent visitor, where she could sit in the comfort of her own room in the grandstand. She liked her food, and she had to be fed on the hour.

She got into trouble with the Windsor stewards on one occasion when her Broad Atlantic showed great improvement compared with its two previous starts to win at short odds. They were dissatisfied with the explanations of the owner, jockey, and trainer's representative and referred the matter on to the National Hunt Committee. After an hour and a half with them, explanations about Broad Atlantic were accepted,

Bacardi wins the Bucks and Berks Handicap in June 1940.
Note the judge's new box in the background

Trying to get in, May 1944 (Getty Images)

Once inside.... (Getty Images)

(Getty Images)

but one imagines Miss Paget made her views on the whole matter pungently clear. Later that year she removed her horses from trainer Walter Nightingall's yard.

Miss Paget was, however, the owner of several good horses including the multiple Cheltenham Gold Cup winner Golden Miller, and the 1940 victor Roman Hackle, who had run at Windsor. Whatever prize money they earned, her large string of horses were valuable in helping to keep racing activity and standards up during the war, when many other owners had other priorities.

***

That Easter Monday in 1943 Carey also rode an up-and-coming sprinter called Sugar Palm, but many of those present will have remembered it as the day that they saw Gordon Richards overtake Fred Archer's nineteenth century record of the most career winners when he rode his 2,750th on Scotch Mist. Richards, who had been a household name for over ten years and was to be champion jockey 26 times, was loudly applauded for his tremendous achievement. In hindsight Scotch Mist was a very appropriate name. It transpired that Archer's total was actually 2,748, and Richards had passed that total before this Windsor meeting.

Sugar Palm, a five-year-old, won at Windsor again in July and was now on a terrific roll which saw him rise to the rank of champion sprinter. He had won the Stewards Cup the year before (Windsor hosted this famous Goodwood race from 1942-45), and he became one of the select band to win it a second time while amassing six victories from seven starts in 1943. He then pitched up at Windsor on 16 October for the Championship Cup over five furlongs.

Although it cannot quite be compared to the modern Champions Day at Ascot, it was the last meeting of the season and everybody was trying to earn their winter corn. There was also a rare appearance by a jockey even more prolific than Gordon Richards. 61 year old Sam Heapy rode Newfoundland, who did not contribute to the total of 3,260 winners that he rode – and a similar number trained. A nephew of the Loates brothers who rode at the turn of the century, he emigrated to Belgium early in his career, where the vast majority of these winners accumulated.

Eight races on the card attracted an average of 20 runners, but in the Cup only two took on Sugar Palm, the 8/13 favourite. Mehrali had been soundly beaten by him before and was unconsidered at 100/7. At 13/8 Linklater was a dangerous opponent, a really speedy sort but one who, it was thought, would set a strong pace and thereby set the race up for Sugar Palm, who was better over six furlongs. Greatly though the contest was anticipated, it turned out to be thoroughly unsatisfactory. Linklater went off in front as predicted, but Tommy Carey, riding the favourite, found himself boxed in on the rail when Mehrali moved up to challenge the leader. Instead of pulling out wide, he waited for a gap, but none appeared. Mehrali appeared to win by a head, but the judge called Linklater the winner. With a clear run Sugar Palm ought to have beaten them both.

The opening day of the 1944 flat season at Windsor was Easter Monday and once more huge crowds came, with all forms of transport pressed into service including ponies drawing carts, which gave the car parks a particularly varied appearance. Enterprising types used their own little boats or punts to ferry people to the races, making sure that they had collected the fares well before reaching dry land. A queue a mile long formed at the entrances. When the supply of tickets for Tattersalls ran out, the gates were rushed and hundreds got in without paying. There were reports of 5,000 taxis bringing people, and 10,000 bicycles, but they don't correspond with the estimated 20,000 people squeezed into the enclosures, nor with another answer in Parliament from the Minister of Fuel who said there were just 659 taxis present. Once inside, the most assertive racegoers struggled up onto the terracing to get a better view of the action. The highlight of the ten races was the Upper Sixpenny Stakes featuring Dorothy Paget's unbeaten colt Orestes, who had been the favourite all winter for the Derby. Inevitably he was a very short price for this warm-up race, with the Paget purse no doubt forcing his odds down to 1/4. Although he led from the intersection, he was run out of it by the 100/7 shot The Solicitor. As the commentator on the British Pathé newsreel said, it wasn't the first time a solicitor had given people a shock.

Getting home was laborious, with enormous queues for buses and trains. Some people killed time in a pub or a café. Stocks of food and drink were so depleted that several items on café menus the next day would be "off". Two punters were so fed up by the time they'd reached Slough station they crossed over the tracks in order to get to the buffet. A porter ticked them off and when they answered back the police were called. They were fined £2 each for trespassing on the railway.

More serious shocks were felt in the second half of June when the Nazi commanders, seeking a counter-offensive after the D-Day landings gave the Allies a foothold in France, started launching flying bombs (V1s) over south east England. They were pilotless aircraft, each with enough fuel to get to the London area, but nobody could tell where each one might fall to earth. The Chief Constable of Windsor wrote to the Home Office about the effect of a V1 landing on the racecourse populated with a large crowd and the only access being via two narrow bridges. While this could be disastrous, the chances of a bomb landing on the few most densely-crowded acres were very slim, especially as Windsor was twenty miles beyond the prime London targets. The Home Office wasn't very interested but agreed that the public address could be used to give warnings of air raids.

The Chief Constable's concerns looked justified almost immediately. At the 1 July race meeting, just as the runners for the sixth race were preparing to leave the paddock, a warning was broadcast and the sound of the V1, like a cheap motorbike, was heard. It may have been too early in the bombing campaign for everybody to become familiar with the crescendo of the engines of these bombs. If the rumble started decreasing in volume, you were safe; it had passed over and would fall somewhere away from you. The worst outcome for any listener was if the engine ran out of fuel just before the sound reached peak volume; that meant its trajectory was bringing it down very close to you. In ten seconds or so it would hit the ground. Each one had a ton of explosives that could destroy twenty houses in a tightly-packed urban area.

12,000 people were on the course that day. The public address system had been trialled at Windsor the year before, announcing the results and starting prices after each race. Now it was used to warn racegoers about the approach of the V1. If people couldn't take cover they were recommended to lie flat. Assuming it didn't score a direct hit, that would at least reduce the risk of being hit by shrapnel or other debris. There are conflicting accounts of what happened, but the likelihood is the bomb came from the north east and passed over the course as the engine cut out. It glided down onto a disused Council refuse incinerator on Kentons Lane, more than half a mile to the south of the course. Over 300 buildings were damaged. Miraculously nobody was killed, though 60 people were injured by flying glass. Nobody was hurt on the racecourse, ignoring the probably-apocryphal story of the jockey who'd dived to the ground only to be flattened by a large trainer doing the same and landing on top of him.

In the spirit of the stiff upper lip and "keep calm and carry on", once the explosion at a safe distance had been heard people got to their feet, emerged from underneath tables or from any other shelter they could find and got on with the racing. The 3.30 was off only four minutes late. Normality resumed quickly, as Gordon Richards rode the odds-on favourite Travel On to win. As was the custom during the war, the reporting of details of where bombs fell was kept to a minimum so as to prevent the enemy from benefiting from the information. The report of the day's racing in The Times only referred to it via the opening sentence, which was, "There was an usually exciting day's racing at Windsor".

After The Solicitor had surprised in April he disappointed in June by finishing second in the Monarch Stakes, the last trial for the Derby in 1944's truncated programme of racing. He was unfancied for the big race, again run at Newmarket, and finished down the field.

However, he returned to Windsor soon after to upset the odds on another red hot favourite, the leading miler Fun Fair, which showed how unreliable The Solicitor could be. Meanwhile Dorothy Paget's Orestes ducked the Monarch Stakes before being unplaced in the Derby, only to regain some kudos by scrambling home in the City Bowl, Salisbury's most famous race, which was run this year at Windsor – another case of it staging other courses' important flat races.

Sugar Palm, who finished second to Mehrali half an hour after the V1 dropped, was beaten a short head three weeks later when odds on and conceding 30 pounds to the winner, and reached the pinnacle of his career in August by taking the Nunthorpe Stakes, the established championship race for sprinters, which had been transferred from York to Newmarket. He didn't care for its fast going and its undulations but overcame his dislike with his trademark late run. He was helped by the starter letting them go when one of his principal rivals was standing sideways at that moment, and another, Mehrali, stuck behind that one.

He had a hard race at Ascot before enjoying his seventh success at Windsor in October, to the delight of the crowd. He lost several lengths due to being bumped in the first part of the race but a now-obligatory barnstorming finish carried him across the line a head and a short head in front of his closest rivals. There was no criticism of the judge's verdict. Sugar Palm was brought out again when Windsor hosted the last day of the season on Saturday 4 November, but he could beat only 19 of his 20 rivals. The other one, Boston Stump, carrying 39 pounds less, hung on by a neck. The attendance was the biggest ever seen other than on a bank holiday weekend, thanks to Sugar Palm, plus a growing feeling that with the Allies pushing further into France, the war was nearer the end than the beginning.

This optimism took tangible form with the announcement that National Hunt racing could be resumed. Despite there being no materials or labour with which to build hurdles and fences, and half of the jumps tracks being ploughed up, Windsor was ready to go on Boxing Day 1944, when it and Wetherby were due to stage the first jump meetings since March 1942 and the first of those at Windsor since

March 1940. Bad weather intervened and that meeting, as well as the next two, was abandoned. It wasn't until 10 February that the severe conditions abated and racing could go ahead. Then it was a case of feast after famine; 191 horses competed in eleven races, the most for a National Hunt meeting for over thirty years. One of the runners was Sugar Palm. As if being champion sprinter wasn't enough, he was tried over hurdles in the winter, but to no effect. Two of the day's winners, Red Rower and Brains Trust, took the Cheltenham Gold Cup and the Champion Hurdle the following month. For Red Rower, now aged eleven, it was deserved compensation for finishing third in 1941 and second in 1942. The cessation of jump racing for two and a half years while he was in his prime limited what might have been a fine career.

The feature of the next Windsor meeting, two weeks later, was the Boveney Chase, with three Gold Cup contenders, Paladin, Schubert and Poet Prince. There was an exciting finish, Poet Prince finishing fast and late, but the Gold Cup winner of 1941 could only finish second by a neck to Schubert. That day there were 175 runners. These fixtures were much appreciated by jockey Tommy Isaac, who rode three winners at the first meeting and four at the next. The groundstaff weren't so happy. The turf was so badly cut up the next two meetings were cancelled and transferred, to allow it to recover in time for the flat season. The resident billy goat who helped keep the grass down in ordinary times was not needed.

Steel had built a bar on the site of the current Paddock Pavilion for owners, trainers and jockeys during the war, but it became popular with the Steels and one end of the building became the "family bar". with guests including Dr May, effectively the GP for the Castle and Eton College, and the butler Aitken on hand to tend to their needs.

As the war in Europe came to its conclusion Windsor was allocated a number of flat meetings for the summer of 1945. Normality began to return. Disputes about close finishes resurfaced. Sugar Palm ran gallantly, but with less success. The handicapper and then Anno Domini caught up with him. He died in 1950 on the gallops, aged twelve, having won 22 of his 78 races. On a happier note, Bindi Steel was married at St Andrew's church in Clewer but her wedding reception was held at the course. That was a most unusual venue for 1945, and while understandable from a sentimental point of view the presence of a good stock of alcohol in the cellar cannot have been a disadvantage.

CHAPTER 9
CHURCHILL

John Knight had quickly overcome those early administrative setbacks and once his organisational ability shone through and the racecourse's financial situation had improved Henry Steel appointed him as managing director in 1941. Knight was also an accomplished pianist who gave classical music recitals in London. In 1943 he became a founder member of the Royal Windsor Horse Show and served on its committee. That same year he introduced free racecards, handed out by nurses with collecting boxes for the local hospital, which raised thousands of pounds in the next five years.

Hoping to avoid falling back into the old pre-war pattern of racing and the mediocrity that Windsor had been known for, he tried to improve quality by putting good prize money into new races, like the patriotically named £750 Waterloo Stakes and the £1,000 Victory Handicap. However, his efforts were repaid with small fields. The Stewards Handicap for £1,000 was the last replacement Stewards Cup. He introduced a marathon flat race, the Long Walk Stakes, over two and a half miles, and in 1947 a Long Walk Handicap Hurdle. Suitably, but unusually for those days, it was over three miles. The hurdle race title was commandeered by Ascot when they introduced jumping in 1965.

After the war Knight's oldest son Jack joined the racecourse staff. It must have seemed tame for the lad. Born in 1922, he joined the RAF early in the war and saw more than his share of aerial action. He had two tours of 20 missions each – anti-submarine warfare at first, and later with Bomber Command flying over France, which involved more being shot at. Then he was told he had to do a third tour. Eventually he flew one mission too many and his plane was shot down over Berlin. Of the nine crew members, he was one of two to survive. The Germans detailed him to help pick bodies out of bombed buildings before being sent to a prisoner of war camp for two years. Fortunately he was quite well treated and the main problem was bad food, and he lost a lot of weight. Years later he admitted that the worst moment of the war was when his camp was liberated by a horde of drunken Russian Cossacks, who rampaged through it in an orgy of violence. He and a friend managed to sneak away undetected, get back to the Allied lines and returned to England in mid-1945 to a hero's welcome from the family.

The fixture list would not regain a semblance of normality until 1946, when more courses were derequisitioned by the authorities. Accordingly, Gold Cup types such as Red Rower and Medoc II (the 1942 winner) could still be seen in action at Windsor in the winter of 1945/46. Fred Rimell rode four winners on 8 December, one of which was the 15 year old Rightun, who in building up a run of four victories himself was representative of a number of old horses who had been brought back into training as the supply of younger ones had been interrupted by the war.

Windsor stood in for Kempton to supply racing on Boxing Day 1945. The three-runner selling chase provided great amusement. The favourite's race ended when he fell at the first. Roman Law made it to the water jump before coming down. Left alone, Never Mind II got to the fourth last, where he refused repeatedly. The remounted Roman Law caught him up and they both refused. Roman Law kept trying, to no avail, while Never Mind II's jockey Stothard gave up and returned to the paddock. Never Mind II's owner-trainer Mr Brunt clearly did mind, for he sent horse and jockey back to the fourth last to try again. Success! They got over it, only to capsize at the second last. Quickly Stothard caught the horse, remounted, jumped the last and won the race. This two mile race had taken eleven and a half minutes, seven more than normal.

Chaka won the Herne The Hunter Chase, his fourth course win that year. He had blossomed when switched to front running tactics, and by virtue of his good jumping became a favourite with the Windsor regulars. He was entered for the Gold Cup and the Grand National, only for injury to sideline him for a year. Nevertheless he'd taken his course tally to seven by December 1948, when he was nearing his twelfth birthday. He nearly blotted his copybook in a three-horse race gifted to him by his inept opponents. Bright Boy fell, and Singlestick blundered into the open ditch in front of the fence. After being remounted, Singlestick did the same again. Chaka, all on his own, disgraced himself by refusing a fence out in the country three times – one that he'd jumped with no qualms numerous times before. Bookmakers were by now offering odds about there being no finishers. Eventually Chaka consented to jump the fence and completed the course, full of running, for win number eight. There'd been so many fallers that day the groundsmen had to stay late to lower the height of the fences for the second day of the meeting. Though Windsor's fences were not normally regarded as stiff, there had always been quite a few fallers there. One theory put this down to horses getting unbalanced if they couldn't change legs to cope with the alternating right and left bends.

There was another course specialist whose appearances delighted Windsor racegoers in the post-war years. Lord Stalbridge's Red April, a half-brother to Red Rower, won eight chases at Windsor from 1945-50. He won another eight at Wincanton, his owner's local track, where a race was named after him. Red April enjoyed a long, consistently successful career, for between winning the County Hurdle at Cheltenham in 1942 and the ultra-valuable Queen Elizabeth Handicap Chase at Hurst Park nine years later when aged 14, he had been third in the Champion Hurdle and the Gold Cup in successive years.

Since Red April and Chaka won eight each just after the war no jumper has won more than five times at Windsor. Others who have scored five times are Bundu and Hindhead (1957-65), Even Up, the Daily Mirror Punters Club horse, and King Kong (both 1973-77), Straight Accord (four of those wins coming in two months in 1984) and Avonburn (1992-94).

Six out of nine days' scheduled National Hunt meetings were

lost due to the exceptionally harsh winter of 1946/47. Once the long-lying snow melted, there was severe flooding. The racecourse buildings were under three feet of water – the table in the stewards' room was found bobbing up and down. £10,000 worth of damage was done. Out on the track, only the tops of the steeplechase fences were visible. As Knight ruefully observed to Peter O'Sullevan, "It's a shame, because underneath all that the going's perfect." As a result of that a new weighing room with offices was built in 1950-51, with steps leading up to them so that the most important parts of that building wouldn't be disabled by future floods. The architect, Lt-Col Douglas Wallis, was a racehorse owner and his design incorporated a substantial enlargement of the paddock. The saddling boxes alongside the pre-parade ring date from this time. Wallis's father's practice, Wallis Gilbert and Partners, had been acclaimed in the inter-war years for their design of the Hoover and the prematurely demolished Firestone Tyre factories in west London.

After the war there was so much rebuilding to be done nationwide that materials and permission to build were in short supply, which accounts for the delay. The old stands had to make do with being patched up – and lasted forty more years. Perversely, after the floods the summer of 1947 was a hot one and in August thousands of gallons of water were pumped from the Thames onto the track to try and take the sting out of the hard going.

Two-legged favourites seen in the late 1940s included the multiple champion jockey Gordon Richards, who often picked up winners at Windsor, the highlight being a four-timer in August 1946. Gordon's brother Cliff was also a jockey, and they gave each other no quarter when it came to riding winners. One afternoon Cliff objected to Gordon for crossing in front of him, but it was overruled. Later he rode at his most determined to beat Gordon, which was spoilt only because somebody else finished in front of both of them.

The gallant Lord Mildmay rode his Cromwell to victory at Windsor in 1949. Mildmay had wretched luck twice in the Grand National when riding his own horses. Davy Jones ran out before the last when in the lead in 1936 when Mildmay's reins came apart, and he was struck by cramp at the Canal Turn when riding Cromwell in 1948 and was unable to lift his head up. Despite that he kept going and finished a close third. The year after he won at Windsor he disappeared after going for a swim in the sea. It was presumed that another attack of cramp had incapacitated him and he had drowned.

The most notable visitor of all at this time was the former and future Prime Minister, Sir Winston Churchill. After Labour's decisive victory in the first post-war General Election, Churchill was forced to move to the sidelines as Leader of the Opposition. This must have seemed like thin gruel after leading the country through the war. In the first part of 1949 his son-in-law Christopher Soames felt Churchill needed a fresh interest that wouldn't cause undue exertion; he was in his 75th year.

Churchill had been in the cavalry as a young man, rode in a few military steeplechases and played polo, so when Soames heard of a grey French-bred racehorse called Colonist II that had recently joined the Epsom yard of Walter Nightingall, and might be for sale, he suggested that Churchill should buy it. The purchase was agreed in the spring of 1949 and Churchill registered his own racing colours before amending them to pink with chocolate sleeves and cap, the same as those of his father Lord Randolph. They had been carried to victory in the 1886 Oaks by L'Abbesse de Jourrare (commonly mispronounced as "abscess on the jaw"). much to the surprise of Lord Randolph, who had gone fishing.

Colonist II's first race for his new owner was a winning one on 25 August. Ridden by Tommy Hawcroft, he made all the running at Salisbury. Churchill couldn't be there, as he was recovering in the south of France from a minor stroke, but two weeks later he was on the mend and decided to purchase two more horses. Colonist II was brought to Windsor for the Lime Tree Stakes over a mile and a quarter on 10 September. It was a sunny afternoon, and hopes were high for another victory. Churchill was well enough to come and he, his wife Clementine and other members of the family admired the good-looking grey in the paddock before settling into the royal box to watch the race through their binoculars. To their delight and that of the crowd, Hawcroft brought the 1/5 favourite home eight lengths ahead of his four opponents. Everyone hurried over to the winner's enclosure to see Colonist II greeted by his happy owner. A few weeks later the horse won a bigger prize at Ascot even more impressively.

Colonist II turned out to be an excellent purchase, for in 1950 he won eight of his nine races, his colour, front-running style and will to win making him and his owner more popular every time. Earlier in Churchill's political career, when he was Chancellor of the Exchequer, he was widely criticised for the introduction of the betting tax in 1926, which led to the strike by bookmakers at Windsor described above. Though the tax was watered down prior to being abolished, it didn't do his reputation any good at the time. But this was all long forgotten. The horse went on to win 13 of his 23 races, one of them being the Winston Churchill Stakes at Hurst Park. He'd also been second in the Ascot Gold Cup and fourth in the inaugural King George VI and Queen Elizabeth Stakes. He was retired at the end of the 1951 season, when Churchill had been re-elected as Prime Minister. He sold Colonist II to go to stud, claiming he could not be seen to be living off the immoral earnings of a horse.

It wasn't all wine and roses, though. Hawcroft had been very ill during the war and his health was fragile afterwards. After riding Colonist II to his three wins in 1949 his career faltered and his rides dried up in 1952. Two years later he was found dead in a wood near Banstead. A gun was found nearby. The coroner recorded an open verdict. And though one of Churchill's new purchases, the two-year-old Canyon Kid, won his debut by four lengths at Windsor on 31 May 1950, he only ran once more before being fatally injured on the gallops.

To begin with Clementine was dubious about his involvement in racing, but less so when she saw the passionate interest it generated in him. His love for racing grew so much that Soames once wrote, "Winston is well and wanting to go racing continuously – in fact more often than the horses do."

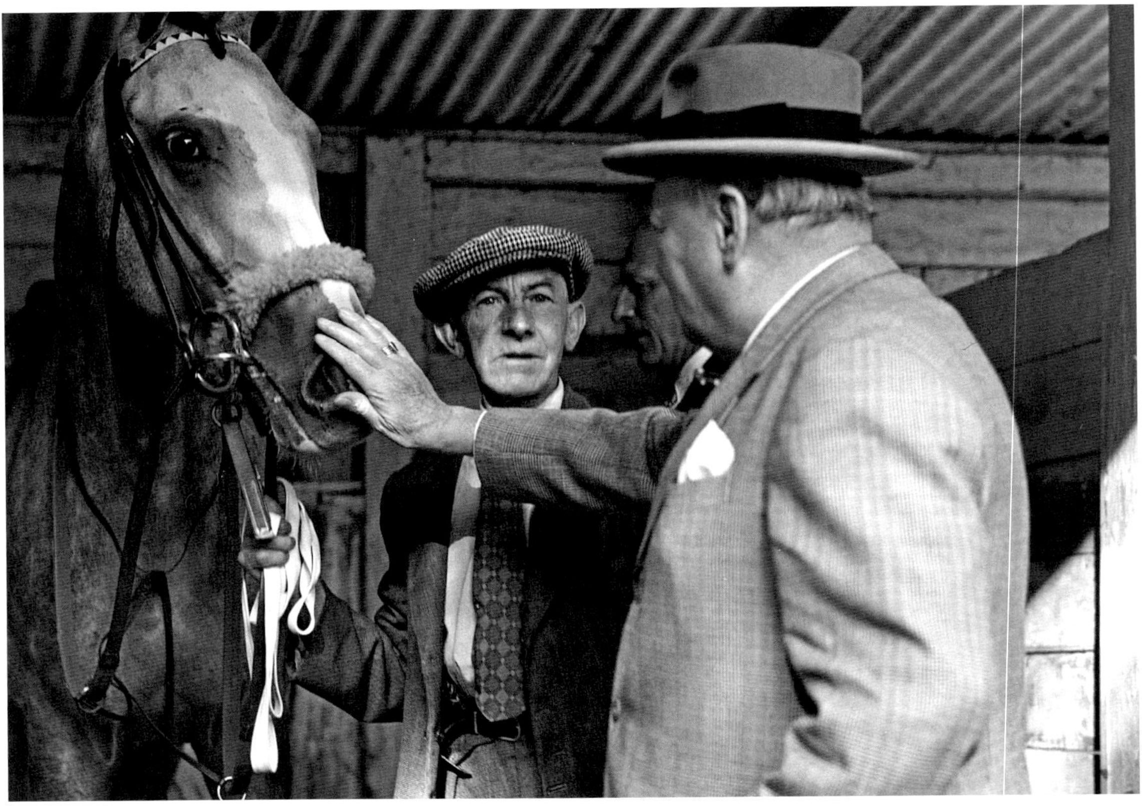

Churchill with Colonist II (PA Images)

The Lime Tree Stakes nears its conclusion (PA Images)

(PA Images)

Greeting Tommy Hawcroft after the race (PA Images)

Walter Nightingall, who'd somehow survived as trainer for Dorothy Paget for eleven years up to the Broad Atlantic incident, found Churchill a rather easier owner to deal with. Nightingall was the third generation of his family who trained from the South Hatch yard at Epsom. He'd had a very brief riding career, fracturing his skull when he was just fourteen in a race at Windsor. A trainer for over forty years, his best horse was the 1943 Derby winner Straight Deal. In fifteen years of racehorse ownership all 36 of Churchill's horses were stabled at Nightingall's Epsom yard. Most were flat racers, but a few went over the sticks and at Kempton on Boxing Day 1952 his hurdler Pol Roger became the first horse owned by a Prime Minister to win a National Hunt race. A few punters who had seen Campari win earlier that afternoon hopefully latched on to the alcoholic double. In November 1963 the juvenile hurdler Sun Hat became his only winner over jumps at Windsor.

Churchill had other successes there on the flat. On 30 May 1957 he had a double; first Holiday Time scraped home after making all the running, and then Le Pretendant, a 1/9 favourite, comfortably beat one modest opponent. He won the same race a year later. Holiday Time was also to win again at Windsor. Churchill remained interested in racing until his death in 1965, aged 90. His horses had won 71 races between them. Colonist II was much the best, and the pleasure he gave Churchill in that race at Windsor is evident in the photographs of him at the races that day, when he realised he had struck gold with this first horse.

CHAPTER 10
OWNERS' TRIBULATIONS

The joys of being a successful owner can be few and far between. An analysis of Windsor's post-war jump races revealed that 24,000 runners contested 2,000 races and the winners were the property of 1,500 different people. The mathematical theory isn't perfect, but it broadly suggests that the average owner had roughly a one in twelve chance of winning, and only a one in four chance of visiting that coveted spot in the winner's enclosure a second time. The trials and tribulations of being responsible for a horse are many and varied.

Little did Windsor racegoers realise the danger they were in when Bistor ran third here at the beginning of March 1950. He had shown signs of waywardness at the finish of a novice hurdle at Sandown, which led to his disqualification. During his Windsor race he tried to bite one of his rivals. His trainer Robert Bates lost his licence as a result of this, although it seems a draconian punishment, especially as the horse was allowed to stay in training. He moved to Tom Gates, but after he won at Fontwell in November he ran amok amongst the crowd and savaged the jockey-trainer Bill Marshall. Severe methods were needed to bring him to heel, and as a consequence of this display he was permanently banned from racing.

The Queen (then still Princess Elizabeth) already had a two-year-old filly called Astrakhan, a wedding present from the Aga Khan. Her early work on the gallops suggested she was not very good, and to ease the royal disappointment Lord Mildmay encouraged her and her mother to acquire another horse with proven form as a replacement. Perhaps he had heard of Churchill's new purchase, for it is curious that both they should enter racehorse ownership at the same time. The Queen and Queen Mother tasted their first Turf success when their jointly-owned Monaveen won at Fontwell in October 1949. Astrakhan belatedly showed some prowess at home and won her maiden soon afterwards. She became the Princess's first runner at Windsor when running in the Upper Sixpenny Plate at the end of March 1950, coming in third. It soon became apparent Astrakhan was moderate, but at least she had won a race, and with that she was sent to the paddocks.

The formerly promising Zucchero had become thoroughly unreliable in the second half of his two-year-old season, often refusing to line up or to start. His owner Mr Steuart decided to cut his losses and he changed hands for a modest amount. Imagine his frustration when Mr Rolls, his new owner, immediately reaped a reward when the horse won the 1951 Blue Riband Derby Trial at Epsom. He threw away any chance he might have had in the Derby by getting left by six lengths, to the chagrin of his fifteen-year-old jockey, having his first ride in the race, one L Piggott. Then Zucchero won again before coming to Windsor in July and smashing the mile and a half track record by 1.6 seconds. Later in the month he finished a close second in the first running of the King George VI and Queen Elizabeth Stakes, with Colonist II not far away.

Peter O'Sullevan had owned horses since the war and his first winner, Pretty Fair, was in a Windsor seller worth £186 in March 1954. He had £20 on at 7/2 but lamented that after buying the horse in for 110 guineas, paying the owner of the second £50 – as was the custom then, to guarantee that he would not bid – and incurring other necessary expenses, he still lost £14 on the day. Not until the 1960s when he bought Be Friendly, and Attivo in the 1970s did O'Sullevan get horses good enough to run and win at the big Saturday meetings that he would commentate on for the BBC. Attivo ran a couple of times at Windsor, including his inauspicious racecourse debut in June 1972. On a later occasion he ran reasonably well and O'Sullevan enquired with a bookmaker about a price for a big race six weeks hence. So fearful were the oddsmakers of O'Sullevan's canny betting that before long there were reports of "a massive ante-post gamble" and Attivo was the favourite.

Injury had forced Gordon Richards to retire from the saddle, having achieved a long-awaited Derby victory at the 28th attempt on Pinza in 1953. Dorothy Paget had long planned to send horses to Sir Gordon, as he was by 1955, when he set up as a trainer. She was keen to make sure his first runner was a winner, and she transferred The Saint, one of her two-year-olds trained in Ireland who had already shown distinct promise, to his Wiltshire yard. He was declared to run in an early-season race at Windsor, and despite the absence of racecourse form was made favourite. The Saint won, ears pricked, with the crowd roaring him on from a quarter of a mile out. Horse and trainer were given a rapturous reception when they entered the winner's enclosure. Everyone, except perhaps the bookmakers, was happy.

As journalist Quintin Gilbey recalled, Sir Gordon would occasionally say, "I think we might win a nice race with so and so," to which she would reply, "Nice race my foot, we'll run him at Folkestone and Windsor." Fittingly, Paget's last winner in England was at Windsor in December 1959 when David Nicholson rode Admiral's Lodge to run a juvenile hurdle. She died aged 54 next year of heart failure, exacerbated by a lifetime of heavy smoking and overeating.

In the 50s Gold Cup and Champion Hurdle winners Four Ten, Linwell, Mont Tremblant, National Spirit, Sir Ken and Gay Donald ran at Windsor, as did Halloween, a popular horse who won a host of good races and was placed four times in the Gold Cup. There were also occasional appearances by Lester Piggott in hurdle races. His battles to keep his weight down are well known but as a teenager a career over jumps, where the weight range is higher, was briefly a possibility. He rode 20 winners over hurdles in all, three at Windsor in 1954, 1957 and 1959. The last two were for Teasy-Weasy Raymond, the high-profile hairdresser who part-owned the subsequent Grand National winners Ayala and Rag Trade.

Windsor had enjoyed its last "Saturday after Ascot" meeting in 1947. In 1950 the four days of Royal Ascot were for the first time topped off with the Ascot Heath meeting on the Saturday, a non-royal affair. In 1958 Windsor had a Saturday meeting before Royal Ascot, so it was now an opportunity for punters to get in funds for the big meeting rather than recover them. Big prize money was laid on for meetings in August 1959 and June 1960, including four £1,000 races, but it was halved for the corresponding fixture in 1961. As happened just after the war, higher prize money couldn't be sustained and racegoers kept on coming, regardless of the quality of racing.

Friday 28 and Saturday 29 January 1955 saw the first televised racing from Windsor on the BBC. ITV planned to show racing three times in 1955/56 National Hunt season only for bad weather to intervene. One of those was a foggy day when the start had been delayed and crowd not let in till 1.00, with the first race put back to 1.30. The fog thickened after that race and the rest of the card was abandoned. The disenchantment of racegoers (there being no refunds if a race had been run) grew as they made their way home and found the sun was shining not far away. ITV finally got off the mark on Thursday 1 March 1956. For a time TV was deluged with racing, with all six races being televised from some courses, and John Knight was among those who disapproved, fearing people would stay at home and bet by phone. Gradually a happy medium of televising three or four races per meeting became the norm.

With the legalisation of off-course cash betting and the introduction of betting shops in 1960 came a new duty payable by bookmakers that was channelled into the new Betting Levy Board. This was set up to redistribute funds into the racing industry. Racecourse facilities were generally dire and little modernisation had been undertaken since before the war. Courses were small private companies and it was all too easy for their shareholders to vote for healthy dividends rather than ploughing money back into improvements, especially where the payback, if any, was unlikely to be immediate. The arrival of a body with large sums available in the form of grants and cheap loans signalled a potential bonanza. Nevertheless, the Levy Board expected courses to chip in as well.

Henry Steel had died in 1953 and the chairmanship of the racecourse company passed to his widow, Maisie. In practice it was one of their sons, Tony, who was the most actively involved family

Jack Knight

John Knight in 1918

Jack, John and Eric Knight

member as regards the overall management of the course. Yet it was John Knight, the managing director since early in the war, who was the most public face of Windsor racecourse. At the top of Knight's wish list was a new cheap ring. Windsor already did well with a 7/6 enclosure and he argued that to make racing even more successful he needed to offer really popular prices to get the masses in. Second preference was to smarten up the amenities, and third was higher prize money. By 1963 he had £250,000 worth of plans in mind, but now they involved new stands and filling in the Mill Stream, which if implemented meant the course would no longer be an island. Windsor was not, though, in the Levy Board's list of top priority courses; they had to make do with just £20,250 in the second round of grants for a new cafeteria in the Silver Ring in 1967.

Race sponsorship grew throughout the 1960s, though not so much at Windsor. Gold Cup types were less likely to appear there, being attracted to other courses with more valuable races. Despite that it became a good place to see Grand National winners. Kilmore, Jay Trump, Anglo and Specify won at Windsor in the 1960s. In February 1964 Kilmore ran here while ante-post favourite for the National even though he was aged 14. The much-vaunted novice chaser Dunkirk, for whom great things were prophesied, won twice at Windsor before taking a fatal fall at Ascot. On the first occasion he beat the 14-year-old former champion hurdler Merry Deal, who was being introduced to fences at a very advanced age. The connection with many of these were jockey-turned-trainer Fred Winter and the older trainer Fulke Walwyn, both masters of their art and supporters of Windsor. Between them their yards were to send out over 150 winners at the course.

In January 1965 the Long Walk Hurdle, a handicap, was run for the last time before the race name was absorbed into Ascot's programme for its new jumps course. Windsor used to run the Cumberland Lodge and the Royal Lodge Stakes on the flat (and a Royal Lodge Chase) but those race names have gone to Ascot and Newmarket.

On 29 January 1966 a special Centenary Steeplechase was run to celebrate the 100th anniversary of the National Hunt Committee, jump racing's first regulatory body. A number of courses were awarded Centenary Chases that year, but it was particularly appropriate for Windsor as it was also a hundred years since racing began on Rays Meadow. The Royal Windsor Centenary Handicap Chase was the most valuable National Hunt race ever run on the course and despite competition from the Great Yorkshire Chase at Doncaster on the same day eight potential National candidates ran. The Queen Mother was there to see her Oedipe win it, beating Anglo. She received congratulations from John Knight, who will have pointed out the double anniversary. Gregory Peck's Different Class, a future National contender, won a novice chase in good style that day.

Knight died in April 1966, after working 29 years at the racecourse. The Queen Mother wrote to Jack to convey her sympathy, having known his father for many years. Jack took over, as expected. After his wartime exploits he'd shown the aptitude to become John's deputy at the racecourse. He was a handsome, charismatic figure who took after his father. His younger brother Eric began his career as an accountant with Barclays Bank but he too joined the racecourse team in the early 1950s.

Jack's son Russell worked at the course in the school holidays for pin money and after leaving school was asked to join the payroll temporarily, at a time when head groundsman George Alder and John Knight were unwell. When both failed to recover Jack persuaded Russell to come into what seemed like the family business on a more permanent basis. He joined the groundstaff and before long was in charge and basically ran everything outdoors until his retirement in 2011.

Another of John's legacies was the redesign of the loop at the far end of the course. Actually there were two; one used for steeplechases was long and had a very tight turn; the hurdles and flat loop was rounder. Both straightened up by the six furlong start.

After the changes there was a smaller, round loop for the hurdle and flat races, meeting the sprint course inside the last five furlongs. Today jockeys are still apt to slow down markedly going round that loop, which has a radius of 400 yards, but they must have slammed on the brakes even more with the old tighter one. The starts changed – the old mile used to be by the marina; today's mile start used to be a mile and a quarter. The one mile five furlong opposite the stands became one mile, three furlongs and 150 yards, the longest race on the level. The two and a half mile flat races involving more than one complete figure of eight were discontinued when it was decided that the turn by the winning post was too sharp to take safely at flat racing pace.

Over the years a number of the fences had been repositioned onto the far loop. The thinking was that a lot of the action was therefore hard to view. Races were now being run faster; and there'd been a few falls on the loop, albeit not too serious. The Knights decided, with the help of the Inspector of Courses, to alter the configuration of the fences, and from November 1970 the number of fences at the far end of the track reduced from five to two. The others were rearranged on the nearer loop to fit in with new starting positions. The water jump became the second in the back straight, whereas it had been the first. Mumm champagne gave a methuselah to each of the winning owners at the first meeting on the redesigned course. The unbeaten Bula was a winner that day, as was Chaou II for the Queen Mother.

Two divisions of a novice chase a couple of weeks later were much less happy events. A combination of heavy going and a stiffly-packed first fence caused mayhem, of a sort not seen since just after the war. In the first race three fell at the first and two others were hampered. When they came to the same fence on the second circuit the two leaders slipped up. In the second division six went at the first. Only four out of a total of 29 got round in the two races. Adjustments to the fences and the starts meant this carnage did not recur.

A horse called Sirius III was the novelty in 1967, winning over both hurdles and fences at Windsor as a four-year-old. It was very unusual for a horse of that age to run over the bigger obstacles, even more so than today. He is believed to be the first Russian-bred winner over jumps in this country. He was purchased from the Russian government by Isidore Kerman, the solicitor who later bought Plumpton and Fontwell racecourses and owned several good horses with names that included Kybo, the acronym for the well-meant advice his mother gave him when he went to college.

Flat racing in the 1960s remained steadfastly undistinguished, with a few exceptions. Operatic Society, known for his exploits at Brighton, was good elsewhere and durable. He was ten years old when, to the delight of Windsor racegoers, he won for the 30th time in July 1966. The popular grey handicapper My Swanee won there next summer; he won 17 times in all. His trainer, Bill Marshall, was very keen on the chances of his runner Littleton Lad at Windsor one day in May 1969. He had runners to saddle at Wye in East Kent and needed to get from one course to the other within two and a half hours, which took some doing without the M25 to assist. Marshall had been a fighter pilot during the war and was used to taking risks, so much so that his journey was interrupted by being stopped for speeding three times. He told each of the policemen to back Littleton Lad. Whether he got three tickets is not recorded, but the horse won, which doubtless covered any fines.

For years the evening meetings always seemed to end with a maiden race, and betting on the favourite was the standard ploy to recoup any losses. A three-year-old filly called Park Top made her debut in a Windsor maiden that closed the card on 22 May 1967 and was among the "20/1 others" in the betting. She turned out to be one of the best flat horses to have run at Windsor in the second half of the twentieth century. Not only did she win, following up at Newbury, Royal Ascot and Brighton, but as a five-year-old she cleaned up in a trio of top-grade races, the Coronation Cup at Epsom and Ascot's Hardwicke Stakes and King George VI & Queen Elizabeth Stakes. Park Top was also second in the Eclipse Stakes and the Prix de l'Arc de Triomphe, and some observers believed that with different tactics she might have won them too. Her breeding was unremarkable and she changed hands for 500 guineas as a yearling, yet she earned almost £137,000 in prize money for the Duke of Devonshire. Sadly, as a broodmare she could only pass on the 500 guinea genes and few of her offspring cut much ice.

On 12 May 1969 it was a well-bred three-year-old colt, Habitat, who lined up for his Windsor maiden. He had run down the field at Sandown but a combination of his £105,000 price tag at the Keeneland yearling sales and Lester Piggott being on board accounted for him being made 2/1 favourite in a field of 20. He was beaten a head, but was promptly stepped up in class and won five of his other six races that year. The only one he didn't win was at Royal Ascot when he was up against the 2,000 Guineas winner Right Tack. Habitat was beaten half a length and his rider (Piggott) was suspended for seven days for leaning on the winner. Nevertheless he was the highest rated horse of that year and was sold to go to stud for £400,000, where he bred numerous winners on the track and several of the dams of successful racehorses of the 1980s and 90s.

Piggott's will to win on the track has never been in doubt. He was in trouble with the Windsor stewards another time, before cameras were as numerous as they are now. Willie Carson told a story of Piggott pushing him bodily when his mount was going better entering the final furlong. Carson was so surprised he nearly fell off but still managed to win. Piggott got away with a dressing-down.

Carson's best Windsor performance was when riding four winners at the pre-Royal Ascot evening meeting on 13 June 1977. Nevertheless he wasn't completely happy, because he dropped his whip during the last race, and couldn't find it before it became too dark to search any longer. He was particularly disappointed because it was his "lucky whip". Jack Knight got the groundsmen to look for it the next morning and once they found the whip it was sent over to Ascot. Armed with it, Carson won the Royal Hunt Cup the following day for the Epsom stable of John Sutcliffe, whose runners in big handicaps were feared by the bookies for many years.

While being renowned for his taciturnity, Piggott's status could make him persuasive. On another occasion at Windsor he sweet-talked

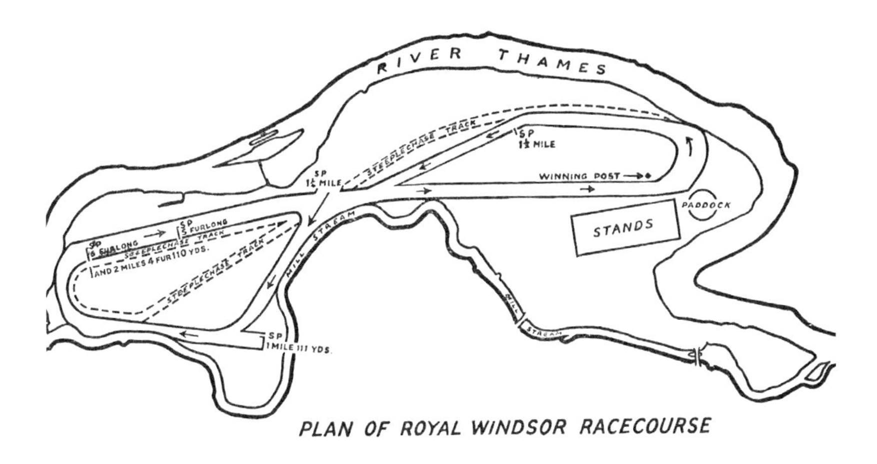

PLAN OF ROYAL WINDSOR RACECOURSE

the stewards into disqualifying an apprentice-ridden filly that had made all the running, his objection being on the basis that the filly had frightened his horse.

Piggott himself had been the victim of a strange hoax in July 1970 while he was being flown from Nottingham's afternoon meeting to ride Abigail Hill for Staff Ingham in the first race at Windsor in the evening. Someone rang Ingham pretending to be Piggott saying he wouldn't get there in time. Half an hour later Ingham had a call from someone purporting to be jockey Eddie Hide, confirming that Piggott would be too late and offering to take the ride. Ingham accepted and said he suspected the first caller wasn't Piggott. But the second caller wasn't Hide, it was another impostor. Nobody knows what the rationale was for this, but Abigail Hall wound up being ridden by yet another jockey into third place.

Flat handicaps at Windsor have always been competitive, so it was a fine achievement by Jack Holt, a trainer known first for jumpers and then for sprinters, to produce his four-year-old grey filly Quortina to win at the course five times in an eight week spell in the summer of 1970. Ostensibly her form was nothing special in the first few months of the season, but Holt knew that starting stalls made all the difference with her. He felt she would have won earlier in the season at Windsor and Goodwood if stalls had been in operation, as advertised. Instead the races she ran in there had the old-fashioned barrier start, whose abrupt raising spooked some horses such as Quortina. She lost 20 lengths at the start of the Windsor race and 10 at Goodwood, where she ran on to finish fourth.

When Holt got to Windsor on 13 July and found the promised stalls were present he was optimistic of a good run and one can only hope he invested something at 25/1. Ridden by the lightweight jockey Bill Jesse, Quortina shot out of the stalls, set a brisk pace, and was all out to win by a neck from Gaberdine, ridden by Lester Piggott. She returned on 1 August and won again, with Ron Hutchinson up. There was no suitable race for her at Windsor's 3 August meeting but there was one at Folkestone, where Geoff Lewis rode her to victory. She returned to Windsor for the four-timer on 10 August, with Hutchinson back on board for this and her next three races.

On the 17th Quortina was back again, but could only finish second. She bounced back with a win on the 28th and another on 7 September to make it 6 wins out of 7 races, all but one at Windsor. Her wins came over a mile and a quarter and a mile and half, either making the running or racing quite near the leaders and she was equally adept at evening or afternoon meetings. A race was named after her, which she won in 1972. It was run in her memory until 1999.

CHAPTER 11
EVENING RACING

The first Windsor evening meeting took place in 1964, fully thirteen years after the original experiment at Manchester. To begin with it seemed that racing at that time of day brought more opportunities for everybody. In May 1957 Tommy Gosling rode the winner of the 3.30 at Windsor before flying to Lincoln to ride two more at their evening meeting, the first of them at 6.45. However, after widespread initial enthusiasm racecourse managers found that attendances were not very different from those in the afternoon, and they dropped alarmingly if the weather was bad. Nevertheless the proprietors of Manchester (until it closed in 1962) and Alexandra Park in north London latched on to racing in the evening as a good way to catch thousands of people living nearby or on their way home from work.

Although the M4 from junctions 5 to 9 was open by 1963, the benefit to Windsor racecourse was limited, for traffic still had to wend its way through the town centre or via Maidenhead, which was almost as busy. What made all the difference was the creation of the A355 spur road from junction 6 in 1966. Its construction meant the racecourse stables in Clewer Court Road had to go; new ones were built next to the Silver Ring.

The racecourse had a hundred-year lease on a right of way through the Mill House grounds and it so happened that there wasn't much time until it expired. When the new stables were completed this short cut from the stables to the track was no longer needed. The resident of Mill House, the actor Michael Caine, paid the racecourse a modest sum to relinquish its right of way ahead of its formal end. The old stables were eventually replaced with housing.

Eric Knight decided evening racing was the way forward, especially as the M4's eventual extension to Bristol was set to reduce travel time to the course considerably for trainers and racegoers throughout central and southern England. Despite its late start in the evening racing stakes, by 1968 Windsor had overtaken Alexandra Park, with ten meetings against the suburban course's eight.

Evening racing was enjoying a resurgence in popularity, but the Levy Board didn't entirely approve. They had to fund more prize money, security services and camera patrols and got nothing in return, whereas the racecourses benefited from the extra gate money. There was less betting on evening meetings, so less levy was collected, and for that reason the Tote also was lukewarm about evening meetings.

Lord Wigg, the Chairman of the Levy Board, undertook to visit all the country's racecourses to see for himself where funds were needed and who deserved them. He noted that Windsor had two dozen fixtures, and more on the flat (17) than any other course except Newmarket and "they appear to run meetings wherever they can be fitted in." Alexandra Park was forced to close on safety grounds in 1970, which allowed Windsor to consolidate its position as the London course for evening racing.

One of Wigg's decisions was to reduce the number of evening meetings, except those at Windsor, Edinburgh & Hamilton, where their quantity (in Windsor's case) or particularly successful events (e.g. the Saints and Sinners charity night at Hamilton) had become an integral part of their fixture list. Other courses would now need to justify the financial necessity for evening meetings.

Windsor capitalised on a story in the popular press in 1971 about Royal Ascot, when women wearing hot pants were refused entry to the Royal Enclosure. Six weeks before, a couple of newspapers had erroneously reported that they would be acceptable if worn as part of an ensemble. The Duke of Norfolk, the Queen's representative at Ascot, corrected this, saying "I wish to make it abundantly clear that the only form of ladies trousers permitted will be suits with long trousers." A contrastingly warm welcome awaited hot pants-wearers at the next Windsor meeting, where they were admitted free if accompanied by a gentleman.

Falls in flat races are rare, but all the more dramatic for being unexpected. Accidents happen from time to time at even the best-run course. One of Lester Piggott's most embarrassing Windsor moments was in May 1974 when falling off Campanologist close to the winning post. He was in the lead at the time and was lucky to escape injury as his 16 rivals, led by the favourite Tamerboy, galloped past. The judge decided he had parted company with his mount before passing the post and declared Tamerboy the winner. Piggott and several others who had backed Campanologist at 4/1 disagreed, but the photo finish camera had broken down and there was no evidence to overturn the judge's verdict. He bounced back with a treble and a four-timer at Windsor meetings later in the year.

Perhaps the most dramatic fall of all was that of Wenallt Red Knight on 23 August 1976, who broke through the rails and careered off the course into the Thames near the intersection, taking his jockey Des Cullen with him. "I thought I was a goner," Cullen said later. "I can't swim and went down three or four times, my feet sticking in the mud. Then a man jumped in and rescued me." That was Roy Clark, one of the groundstaff. Roy probably deserves a book to himself. He first came to work at Windsor at the end of the war aged fourteen, and he still works there one day a week and on race days. Wenallt Red Knight managed to get out of the water after a quarter of an hour. The stewards enquired into the incident and Cullen gave evidence wrapped in blankets, having divested himself of his wet silks and not wanting to keep the stewards waiting while he got properly dressed.

Seven horses came down in a 19-runner Windsor maiden in June 1983. One horse was killed and two jockeys had to go to hospital, but it could have been much worse. In 1992 Barlogan also took a dip in the Thames, and this time stalls handler Mark Wilson boldly waded in to rescue him.

The Queen Mother's horses were virtually all jumpers and although the winter weather could be a deterrent she rarely allowed it to interfere with her desire to go racing, especially if she had a runner. The racecourse management had to be ready for the possibility of her attendance, and at short notice. A phone call might be received from the Castle to say she might come the next day. The caterers, Letheby & Christopher, had to prepare two dishes for her to choose from, one being steak and kidney pie and the other cold ox tongue and salad. She would make up her mind which one to have when she got there. And at three o'clock she would be served Dundee cake and vintage port. Gin and dubonnet was one of her favourite tipples, which Clerk of the Course Hugo Bevan once accidentally spilled over her.

She seldom spoke in public other than at formal occasions but consented to talk to the former champion jockey Terry Biddlecombe one day at Windsor in 1987. He rode in the royal colours many times and piloted the Queen Mother's Game Spirit to victory in the 1974 Fairlawne Chase. This rare interview was the highlight of an ITV documentary about her interest in racing called Royal Champion.

The Royal Windsor Chase (without the Centenary in the title) had become the highlight of the Saturday fixture in late January from 1967 until the 1980s, when it moved to an earlier midweek date. After winning its first running the Queen Mother's Oedipe was second in the next two. Her Majesty won it again with Game Spirit, one of her best horses, in 1973. He was second the year after, giving almost two stone to the winner.

The Fairlawne Handicap Chase, over three miles, was first run in December 1962. It was named after the estate in Kent where the Queen Mother's trainer Peter Cazalet was based. Braving the cold of what was about to be one of the worst winters of the century, she saw her Gay Record finish second. Earlier that year he had smashed the record for the three mile chase course by nine seconds (in a time not bettered for another 23 years). It was run as a handicap worth £272 to the winner until November 1968; a conditions race worth over £1,000 known simply as the Fairlawne Chase was inaugurated in February of that year. Stalbridge Colonist, The Laird and What A Myth, three prime fancies for the Gold Cup, ran but all were beaten by Bassinet. The Queen Mother was there to see her Woodman and Chaou II win two of the supporting races.

More good horses were entered, its prize money was imcreased and it soon became Windsor's most prestigious steeplechase, and an annual feature of ITV's racing coverage in World Of Sport. The Queen Mother favoured the race for her horses and any runners she had increased the chance of her being in attendance, though Game Spirit was her only winner in 1974.

Disqualifications featured in 1972 and 1973. In those two races The Laird and The Dikler were first past the post, but each had clearly caused interference and they were demoted in favour of Cardinal Error and Spanish Steps respectively. However, Cardinal Error hadn't been impeded by The Laird at all; it was Red Sweeney, beaten a head and half a length, who had suffered and would have won with a clear run.

Winners of the Fairlawne are listed in Appendix 1, and those in the 1970s were particularly high class. The race was run three weeks before Cheltenham and was an ideal stepping-stone for the Festival, though admittedly small fields and short-priced favourites were the consequence. Bula was arguably the best of them. A former dual Champion Hurdler, by winning the Fairlawne he proved that he could stay three miles, not far short of the Gold Cup distance. He hadn't been working very well at home and his trainer Fred Winter wasn't sure he should run until John Francome gave him a livener with the whip. From there he was impressive and he was cut to 4/1 favourite for the Gold Cup. He didn't win that, but he did accumulate 34 successes in all.

Francome rode four consecutive Fairlawne winners, Bula (twice) and Border Incident, who were both Gold Cup class, and the 33/1 shot Joint Venture, who capitalised when Silver Buck was brought down.

The creation of a new bank holiday for New Year's Day in 1974 gave the Windsor management the idea of moving a meeting they had on the first Tuesday in January to the bank holiday. For 1975 they acquired not only a meeting on 1 January – and on the day before – but also created a big race as a centrepiece. The New Year's Day Hurdle, worth £2,328 to the winner, was the most valuable hurdle race ever run on the course. The winner, Flash Imp, was a good horse who went on to finish second in the Champion Hurdle to Comedy Of Errors.

Encouraged by this, next season the New Year's Eve fixture was abolished and prize money for the New Year's Day Hurdle was doubled. Enterprise was rewarded with a small yet top class field, and current and future champions battling out the finish. Comedy Of Errors beat Sea Pigeon by a head. The crowd was said to be the biggest in living memory for a jumping card. The 1970s was a golden age for hurdlers and Windsor's new race immediately became an important mid-season target for the best of them (see Appendix 2), especially as prize money exceeded that of Kempton's Christmas Hurdle run on Boxing Day or the day after. Beacon Light won in 1978, with Alverton and Comedy Of Errors second and fourth. Celtic Ryde won the next two runnings.

It was unlikely that two similar races so close together would both survive and Kempton retaliated by increasing the Christmas Hurdle prize money. In 1980/81 it was worth £8,439 to the winner, whereas the New Year's Day Hurdle paid only £5,223. Money talks, and the owners of the very best hurdlers wanted to talk more and more to Kempton. Those just below top-class came to Windsor, as did good crowds, who had no other Bank Holiday racing in the south east of the country. Those who went into the centre of the course and had enough energy could stand by a fence in the home straight and, once the field had passed, dash across to the back straight to stand by another jump there. It was a good way to run off the excesses of the festive season.

By 1972 Tony Steel had taken over as chairman from his mother. The Windsor Racecourse Company, set up in 1904 after John Frail's sons had died, had in effect turned into the parent of the new Windsor Racing Limited, which was given a lease to operate the racecourse. The Racing Limited company included Jack and Eric Knight amongst its shareholders, the first time the Knights had a formal stake in the ownership of the course.

Jack's Holy Grail had been to get a hotel built on the site, which would increase the holding company's value and pave the way for a

The Queen Mother and Dick Francis at Windsor in 1969 (Getty Images)

potential sale. Numerous plans were put together over the years involving hotels, housing or golf courses but objections were always made. The racecourse is within sight of Windsor Castle and permission for any new buildings that would dramatically alter the skyline visible from the Castle was always refused. Jack, who took over as chairman in the 1980s, gradually came to accept that selling the racecourse at a price that recognised the development potential simply could not be achieved.

After various attempts were made to sell the course without permission for a hotel, in 1987 agreement was reached by the shareholders of the two companies to sell to a consortium that included the trainer-brothers Ian and Toby Balding. Financing it was David Thompson, who graduated from working at Smithfield market to becoming a meat wholesaler and then co-founding Hillsdown Holdings, which became one of the biggest food companies in the country. It netted him a total of £298m when he sold his shares.

He and his wife Patricia own the Cheveley Park Stud at Newmarket, a site where horse breeding is believed to have taken place for a thousand years. The couple have owned countless good horses and their distinctive colours of red, white sash and blue cap are often seen at the premier flat courses. However, perhaps the family's most high profile success was in the 1992 Grand National with Party Politics, who ran in Mrs Thompson's colours. It was an extremely topical result, there being a general election five days after the big race.

Windsor had been slated in a 1986 survey of racecourses. The popularity of the course baffled the pundits who loved to list its faults: second rate horses, poor facilities, too much action out of sight or in the far distance, the sun in your eyes looking down the straight in evening meetings (not that that could easily be remedied), traffic jams outside, the difficulty of getting out of the car park, and more expensive to get in than Sandown. The stable yard was a fire hazard and the venerable Tattersalls stand, which missed out on refurbishment after the war, was still there. Jack Knight responded by saying these problems were exacerbated by the large attendances at the evening meetings. It was ever thus at Windsor; you could point to them and say with some degree of justification that while they kept on coming, there couldn't be too much wrong.

The Thompsons' consortium believed they could make money from the racecourse and they were better placed to raise cash for improvements. During the 1990s the course was transformed. The old stand was at last knocked down and on 12 June 1995 the Queen Mother opened the new £1.7m Royal Windsor Stand. Then aged 95, she walked up the stairs to the Churchill suite in the Members' Stand, where she stayed to watch three races, but not the Alan Price concert after. On her subsequent visits she was based in the Paddock Pavilion, and chose to climb the stairs rather than use the lift. For a while there was a special Queen Mother footstool kept for her. The Queen, Princess Anne, Prince Edward and the late Princess Diana have been other royal visitors since the 1990s.

The Members' Stand was refurbished internally, with the dark oak panel staircase receiving special attention. The cosy Jam Stick bar, which has refreshed generations of racegoers, remained. The Paddock Pavilion, a two-storey suite of hospitality boxes beyond the winning post, provided extra capacity for the expanding market for corporate winers and diners.

A more upbeat air about the place seemed to bring a better standard of racing. Two top fillies, Niche and Lyric Fantasy, won their maidens at Windsor on the same day in 1992. Niche went on to win the Norfolk and Lowther Stakes and Lyric Fantasy had an even better season, winning the National Stakes, the Queen Mary, the Newbury Super Sprint and the Nunthorpe beating older horses. Since then it's been automatic for the winners of early-season Windsor two-year-old maiden races to be considered for Royal Ascot. Fewer such contests have been programmed in the first half of 2016, as they are being replaced with an experimental series of races with different conditions in an attempt to improve field sizes. Three-year-old maiden races for the first half of the season can throw up late-developers who can go on to Listed or Group race class.

Windsor's top flat race, the Winter Hill Stakes, was an ordinary race worth £345 confined to three-year-old fillies who had not won a £500 race when first run in May 1965. The Oaks entry Mabel won at odds of 1/5. Named after an area by the Thames between Cookham and Marlow, the Winter Hill's status quickly improved and a string of good horses just below top class won, albeit usually at odds on in small fields (see Appendix 3). Arguably the best winner was Parnell in 1972, who had finished second to Brigadier Gerard in his previous race. For its first 20 years it was run in August or September over one mile three furlongs and 150 yards. In 1984 it was reduced to a mile and a quarter, its current distance, and in 1987 it moved to Windsor's August Bank Holiday Saturday, the last evening meeting of the season. It was promoted to Group 3 status in 1995. Saeed bin Suroor and Sir Michael Stoute are the trainers to follow, each having notched seven victories.

Part of a plot to rig Tote dividends involved Windsor in 1990. A winning 1/10 favourite at Lingfield, Big Finish, paid 11/10 on the Tote, the third suspiciously high dividend in a week. Just before the race the Tote's TV monitors were indicating an understandable £1.10, but a £100 bet on an outsider changed it to £2.10. Seconds before the off someone tried to place £500 on Big Finish at the Tote betting shop at Windsor races. He was turned away, as the shop didn't take bets at Tote odds. He was thought to be part of the plot.

Those who were present on 28 June 1993 saw Lester Piggott's last ever Windsor winner, Barahin in a selling race. His first ever winner, 45 years before, was also in a seller. The maestro had come out of retirement after being jailed for tax evasion and stripped of his OBE. Peter O'Sullevan was a great admirer of Piggott's and told a journalist a story about when he was with The Queen at Windsor races. He sounded out Her Majesty about the possibility of restoring his OBE, but she pointed out he had been "rather naughty". The journalist was naughty too, for he printed that comment of the Queen's verbatim, in direct contravention of protocol.

CHAPTER 12
ARENA LEISURE

Windsor doubled the 1988 New Year's Day Hurdle prize money to £14,000, which was only £5,000 less than Kempton's Christmas Hurdle. They were rewarded by the best winner for years, Celtic Shot, who would go on to take the Champion Hurdle in March and win 17 races in all. Kempton's owners had deep pockets, however, and they upped their race's prize money to £28,000.

Few jump races attracted sponsorship at Windsor. Indeed, Hugo Bevan wrote to 40 organisations to back the 1992 New Year meeting to offset the cost of paying Channel 4 to televise it. None wanted to participate, though in the end three big bookmakers and the Tote chipped in. In an attempt to attract more runners, in 1993 the New Year's Day Hurdle was changed to a limited handicap. The prize money was down to £8,000 and there were no longer any aspirations to make it a race for top class horses.

The quality of the Fairlawne Chase had declined a little in the 1980s and 90s but the roll of honour included the National winner Rhyme'n'Reason and Toby Tobias, runner-up in the Gold Cup and the King George VI Chase. Espy's 1991 win came with the aid of a milkshake, according to his trainer Charlie Brooks. This was the colloquial name for sodium bicarbonate administered by a stomach tube. They did this at his Uplands stable before the horse was boxed up and driven to the racecourse. The effects of the milkshake wore off within hours, so it had to be done as close as possible to the race, but not while on the course. In his autobiography Crossing The Line Brooks stated that it wasn't illegal, unlike in Australia. Espy won easily, and on the only other occasion he used a milkshake on Espy he broke the course record at Newbury.

Bad weather caused the abandonment of the New Year's Day meeting from 1995-97 and by then the writing was on the wall for jumping at Windsor. Attendances were simply too low to make the retention of jumping worthwhile. Excluding New Year's Day, only the Fairlawne Chase fixture made a profit – and there were often one or two abandonments each year whose cost had to be allowed for. There had to be a few months' interval after the flat to prepare the track for National Hunt fixtures. These were before portable fences came into use, so old-style fences had to be built into the ground – and then carefully taken out so that the ground was fully repaired and in good condition for racing on the flat. The cost of maintaining the fences and repairing the ground cut up in the winter in time for the flat (over £100,000 in 1998) made it a no-brainer.

Despite gripes about low prize money, trainers and jockeys liked the track. The average field size of 12 was very good for National Hunt races; it was 15 in novice hurdles. Before new safety limits were implemented at the end of 1993 novice hurdles regularly drew the old maximum of 22 runners. The left and right handed bends made it an educational experience for novices and the long straight gave gallopers a chance to make up ground they might have lost on the turns. It drained well and the going was rarely as bottomless as on certain other courses. The Queen Mother had 27 National Hunt winners at Windsor, the last of which was Easter Ross in 1997, a total exceeded only by Dorothy Paget, who had 41 since 1945. A couple of years later Double Brandy was to be Her Majesty's first and last flat race winner on the course.

The day of the last jumps meeting, 3 December 1998, was cold and damp. There was no great protest from racegoers – the crowd was only 400 up on the corresponding day a year before. Nicky Henderson and Mick Fitzgerald took the two divisions of the Farewell Novices' Hurdle. The last race, the Norwegian Blue Handicap Hurdle, was named by someone with a liking for the Monty Python parrot sketch. Charlie Banker won it easily, which prompted a stewards' enquiry, as he had never been placed before. Trainer Karl Burke – for whom this was his first runner since moving yards to Newmarket – gave a satisfactory explanation, as no further action was taken. After sixteen years as Clerk of the Course, it was an apt moment for Hugo Bevan to retire, although ultimately he stayed on hand through the winter to help out.

After 110 years, jumping on Rays Meadow had ended – or so it seemed.

***

The full width of the track was now available for flat racing and the plan was to rail off the stands side in the summer months to leave fresh ground for the autumn fixtures. Windsor was allocated a new meeting to share the first day of the 1999 Turf flat season with Doncaster, but ironically it was abandoned due to waterlogged ground in the pulling-up area.

On 23 December 1999 it was announced that the Thompsons were to sell the racecourse to Arena Leisure, who were building up their own racing empire. The price was £10m in cash plus £3.6m worth of Arena shares. Windsor's 1998 accounts showed a pre-tax profit of £394,000 and the 167-acre site was valued at £8 million despite the Council saying it was Green Belt and that no hotel development would be allowed.

There had been rumours that Windsor was about to be the focus of a deal. Arena had bought Wolverhampton and Southwell earlier that year, having already owned Lingfield and Folkestone plus hotels and golf courses. Three of those courses staged all-weather racing, which was predominantly a winter activity, and Windsor with its meetings focused on the warmer months would complement them nicely. Graham Parr, its chief executive, had said they were evaluating half a dozen alternatives. Stan Clarke's Northern Racing was equally busy buying racecourses that had been privately owned, believing that his more vigorous commercial approach to their management would yield worthwhile profits. Arena's share price, 10p in the spring, leapt to 74p in early December when news that it had raised £7.9m to fund an acquisition and to £1.18 just before the deal was struck.

Arena now had 18% of the fixture list, which gave them more clout when it came to the increasingly complex world of racing finance. This was becoming more dependent on media rights, primarily pictures beamed into betting shops, and less on Joe Public coming through the turnstiles. Arena could now move meetings to Windsor from its other courses, or vice versa, to make best use of the fixtures owned to the company. The number of Monday evening meetings was soon increased – by 2001 there were 16 in the calendar, with only a couple of Bank Holiday weekends breaking an otherwise continuous sequence. Reviving National Hunt racing was not envisaged.

As often happens when businesses change hands, people at the top change too and Sally Dingle, the racecourse manager for nine years, was made redundant. Friends and former colleagues gathered at Ascot for a surprise party two months later where former chairman Richard Thompson paid tribute to her hard work and loyalty.

The amenities had been improved by the Thompsons and there was no urgent need for major expenditure. The restaurant was packed every Monday with diners enjoying food, drink, good views and racing – and outdoors there was that relaxed Windsor ambience. Nevertheless Arena wanted to take the course further upmarket. Each year a special fundraising dinner was held with auctions and raffles, benefiting charities by over £200,000.

Conference facilities on non-race days and corporate hospitality were growth areas. Windsor's proximity to London, Heathrow and the M4 meant it was well placed to exploit this. For a time buses were laid on to pick up City workers at Liverpool Street and take them to evening meetings via Victoria.

The first three-day Royal Windsor Racing Festival, with consecutive racing on Saturday and Sunday afternoons and Monday evening, was held on 2-4 June 2001. Different audiences were targeted each day, not that there's any reason why people shouldn't go on any or all three days. The dates changed in 2004 to a weekend at the end of June but the Festival is now a fixture in more ways than one.

It's not unusual to hear a few foreign accents at evening

meetings, but any French racegoers on 19 June 2001 may have been shocked when hearing the name of debutante On Coo Lay. This in the anglicised pronunciation of the French word enculez, which means to go away in impolite fashion. This was a slip by Weatherbys, the censors of racehorse names, though they could hardly be expected to know every foreign expletive. On Coo Lay ran fourth that night. She then had 14 races in the next six months, losing them all, and probably thought enculez when she kept on being loaded onto the horsebox to go racing. After a two-year interval she resurfaced in Ireland and eventually won a race there, only to be disqualified later for having run at an unrecognised meeting. Next month another Windsor debutante was called Geespot, by Pursuit Of Love out of My Discovery. Weatherbys were happy to allow that more elegantly contrived name.

One evening racegoers were baffled by the absence of commentary when a race got under way, and were then highly amused by its sudden start during the race and its panting, short of breath delivery. Races had been starting late but had now caught up, and the commentator was chatting to someone when this race began. Realising this, he dashed up several flights of stairs to his box and managed to keep enough breath to describe the closing stages. Afterwards he denied that it was due to some sort of amorous encounter in the box.

A much appreciated, newly sited, wider bridge across the Mill Stream costing £1 million was opened on 25 May 2002, replacing the narrow one by the edge of Clewer Park and the allotments. Getting out of the car park used to be such a problem that a pianist was employed in the Club restaurant to encourage people to linger after the last race, staggering the departures.

The next day 32 racegoers were found to have forged car park tickets, allowing them to evade the £2 entry charge for parking near the stands. There had been complaints at other courses from owners and trainers who'd found their car park full on quiet days. A bag containing forged parking discs was discovered in the Windsor car park. Other counterfeit badges that allowed automatic entry onto the course were also in circulation. This was a time when collusion between gate staff at other courses was not unknown. Cash could be taken from a racegoer at the entrance booth but no ticket was issued. Instead of advancing through the turnstile he or she was directed to an accomplice at a gate and told to say so-and-so in the booth said it was all right to let them in.

Pat Eddery called a press conference at Windsor racecourse in June 2003 to announce his retirement from the saddle at the end of that season. He may have chosen Windsor in view of his numerous winners there, notably the evening when rode four having ridden one at Longchamp in the afternoon. His total of 4,632 flat race winners was bettered only by Sir Gordon Richards.

Zara Phillips and Rory Bremner were among the celebrity riders taking part in a four furlong charity race at Windsor in the summer of 2004. Basil Brush was the star turn on Family Day of that year's Festival, accompanied by Milton Johns, who played his landlord in his TV shows for five years. Johns is an actor by profession but his clear, precise and pleasantly distinctive tones had been heard regularly at Windsor since 2001 when he was appointed as the announcer and auctioneer, roles which he performed at a number of other southern courses. He first became interested in the sport when listening to the racing results on the radio with his father. Entranced by some of the horses' names, he would also look for them in the results section of the newspaper. When he was 12 his father took him to Chepstow races and while his parent was bored by it, young Milton loved it.

On leaving school he went to work at a yard in East Ilsley and planned to be a pupil/assistant to a Lambourn trainer, but when his starting date was put back by three months Johns had to look for other temporary work. He joined a drama group that was putting on The Little Foxes and on the opening night found, to his delight, he was completely devoid of nerves. One thing led to another and he started working for the Bristol Young Vic.

He didn't get back into racing until one day at Sandown in the 1980s. This was when there still used to be up to sixteen meetings on Easter Monday and a dozen on the other Bank Holidays. There were

A scene from the War Horse spectacular in 2014

The Last Race at Datchet (Royal Collection Trust/© Her Majesty Queen Elizabeth II 2016)

The 1869 Windsor Grand Military Steeplechase

Summer racing in 1967 (PA Images)

1998: The last day of National Hunt racing - or so it was thought at the time (Getty Images)

Aerial view of the racecourse with the old loop still visible

Arriving in style

Eric Knight

Al Kazeem winning the 2014 Winter Hill

Racing History wins it in 2015

Frankie Dettori and Jenny Powell

Richard Hannon and Richard Hughes

A P McCoy with rugby's Brian O'Driscoll

Princess Anne congratulates Jamie Spencer after his win on War Alert in July 2014

Another scene from War Horse

The Best of British Festival

Ronnie Scott's Jazz Night

The racecourse is an ideal wedding venue

only six full-time racecourse announcers in that era, plus a number of standbys, and while talking to someone from Racecourse Technical Services, the company that employed them, the RTS man said, "You could do that."

Johns did just that, and developed associations primarily with Brighton, Folkestone, Lingfield (where he presided at 800 meetings), Windsor and Plumpton. At times he was working five or six days a week. One day at Lingfield he was told the auctioneer had lost his voice and that he would have to do the auction after the selling race. When he protested, encouragement was forthcoming. "You're an actor, pretend to be an auctioneer." He played the part to perfection, because a fortnight later he was asked to assume the role permanently. Johns holds the record for the highest auction price achieved at Windsor – 24,000 guineas, ie £25,200 (plus VAT) for Whoateallthepius in 2010. It was a second-time-out Richard Hannon juvenile, ridden by Richard Hughes to an easy four length success. Sadly for the buyer, the horse wouldn't win any of its next 20 starts.

Johns has appeared in countless films and TV programmes since the 1960s. He was in Coronation Street for two years playing shopkeeper Brendan Scott until he was killed off in 1993. He retired from his Windsor role in 2011 but still presides at Plumpton.

A huge redevelopment of Ascot racecourse entailed its closure for 20 months spanning 2004-06. It was already known that the Royal meeting of 2005 would be moved to York when in December 2003 the surprise news emerged that Windsor had been asked to take over some of Ascot's National Hunt fixtures while rebuilding went on. To the joy of jump racing professionals and enthusiasts, two two-day meetings in November and December 2004 were transferred to Windsor, with BBC coverage of every day to boot. In spite of all the announcements to the effect that this was not a long-term arrangement, many harboured hopes that Arena's major shareholder Trevor Hemmings, an avowed supporter of the winter game, would contrive its permanent reinstatement. In the summer of 2004 Windsor was confirmed as the venue for those two jump meetings in 2005 as well, and it was also to host Ascot's Shergar

Cup flat race meeting, though there would be no international jockeys' challenge.

For the return of jumping steeplechase fences were borrowed from Worcester and hurdles from Ascot. The going was ideal, good to soft, on Friday 17 November 2004. The day was cold but fine, and with no winner returned at greater than 7/2 punters were happy. The popular grey Monet's Garden won the feature Ascot Hurdle over two and a half miles. More flocked to the course the next day, only to endure constant rain.

By far the highlight of the brief winter jumping programme was the Long Walk Hurdle at the December meeting, a far cry from the race of that name last run at Windsor in 1965 worth £274 to the winner. Ascot had turned the Long Walk into one of the most important mid-season long distance hurdles, and the crack French horse Baracouda had won the last three runnings as well as two Stayers' Hurdles at Cheltenham. For most of his career he was ridden by his trainer's son Thierry Doumen, whose prowess in the saddle invariably attracted criticism even though he rode him to 16 victories in 21 races. By this time Doumen had retired from race-riding and A P McCoy took over as his jockey. In a slowly-run race that hadn't been run to suit him, Baracouda cruised into the lead before the last flight and slowed up after it, thinking he'd done enough. In an exciting finish Crystal D'Ainay and Rule Supreme got to within a length of one of the best staying hurdlers for many years.

The paddock was enlarged by 50% in time for the 2005 flat season, while a £12m redevelopment plan, including replacement of the old stand and the weighing room, and the inevitable hotel, was being prepared – to no avail.

There was an element of anticlimax to the jump meetings at the end of 2005. The November Saturday was abandoned due to frost. Then Baracouda was accidentally not declared for the Long Walk on 17 December, depriving everyone of a chance to see him clash with the new Stayers' Hurdle champion Inglis Drever. Even worse, an unexpectedly sharp frost that didn't start until 6am hardened ground that was cut up from Friday's racing. After two inspections racing was called off at 11.00, by which time many people were already on their way to the track. Acambo, in Friday's finale, the Q Equine Limited Handicap Hurdle, therefore became Windsor's last winner under National Hunt rules. For the umpteenth time Arena representatives explained that the return of jumping wasn't on the cards as it would be commercially impractical – unless they had good quality racing and enough days to make it worthwhile to rebuild the jumps track.

Windsor proved an unlikely substitute for Doncaster in 2006 by staging the last meeting of the Turf flat season, including the £32,000 November Handicap. Richard Hughes rode the winner, Group Captain, on a day when every favourite was beaten.

Clement Freud observed that when his Eau Good beat a horse of the Queen's at Windsor on 23 April 2007, "Not too often does the combined age of the proprietors of the Exacta add up to 163". Happily he had a substantial each way investment at 28/1. This may have been in his mind when he nominated his favourite London area course in the Racing Post. "My vote goes to Windsor, where you can almost feel the value for money. Good food in the restaurant and a plethora of commendable franchises, from bacon butties via Oriental noodles, fish and chips, home-made fudge, ice creams and Icelandic burgers to the Pimm's marquee. And they go to considerable trouble to ensure that people have somewhere to sit, unlike Royal Ascot, where I paid £60 to stand in a queue and be denied access to the elevator and get out of the rain." The variety of food available from mobile catering outlets on summer evenings is remarkable.

The freehold of the adjacent marina and caravan park were sold in 2008/9 for £1.75m. The construction of the marina had been one of Eric Knight's ideas and brought in useful rent income from its operator. Its sale paid off some of Arena's outstanding loans. In 2010/11 a new office building was constructed about a hundred yards before the main entrance. This allowed more of the weighing room complex to be devoted to jockeys and race day officials. Top jockey Hayley Turner put its roof to good use in an unexpected way one fine day by going up on it to sunbathe. The new office building also incorporated an outlet for selling fish and chips that has proved very popular with racegoers, as anyone who has sampled the generous portions will testify.

CHAPTER 13
THE RECORD BREAKER

There was late-season drama in 2011 when jockeys threatened to strike at Windsor and Pontefract on 17 October in response to Richard Hughes's decision to hand in his licence, which in turn came as a result of two bans in quick succession for misuse of the whip. The latter was invoked when he struck a horse six times in the final furlong of a race when the rules dictated a maximum of five. The strike was averted when the British Horseracing Authority agreed to urgent talks with the Professional Jockeys' Association over the controversial new rules, which were subsequently eased. However, there was unrelated uproar at Windsor and on the betting exchanges when the judge called Vimiero the winner of the ten furlong handicap before deciding to call for a photo and then realising that Discoteca was in fact the short-head winner. Confusion was prolonged by his announcement of "number six, Discoteca," whereas Vimiero was number six.

Yet more whip controversy occurred in May 2012 in a Windsor apprentice race that was the first in a new series that restricted use of the whip to waving and being used in the backhand position. The two young riders who fought out the finish breached these rules very obviously throughout the final furlong, and received bans from the local stewards in spite of their claim, backed up by others, that nobody had told them about the unusual limitations of the whip's use in this series. The bans were later quashed.

In 2006 the racecourse car park had been used for the World Rowing Championships at Dorney Lake, on the north side of the river. For its last three days ferries carried 10,000 people a day across the river. In 2012 Eton Dorney, as it was officially called then, hosted the London Olympics rowing events. This time a temporary bridge was built from the racecourse across the river to accommodate an estimated 30,000 daily visitors. Though this meant no horse racing could take place for four weeks, at least huge numbers came through the racecourse gates and hopefully some will have come back for the non-aquatic races. This was after local residents had protested about ten foot high banners bearing the face of betting pundit John McCririck promoting the racecourse as a transport hub for Olympic events.

Nearly all jockey have their armchair critics, and the champions are not immune. Richard Hughes was a man with whom punters had a love-hate relationship. Often he clearly preferred riding a waiting race and coming from behind, and if that failed it would be his fault and not that of the horse. However, on some courses, notably Goodwood and Windsor, he was the man to follow, in more ways than one. At the Thames-side course he liked to make the running. In his autobiography A Weight Off My Mind he divulged his tactics in the longer races. "You take plenty of bends at Windsor, and if you're in front leaving one you can ask your mount to quicken at a point when everything else is still on the turn and therefore unable to instantly respond. It works time and time again."

Hughes famously rode seven winners there on the eight-race card on Monday 15 October 2012. It's almost forgotten that one day in June, riding at two meetings, he collected three winners and seven second places, and in September he rode six winners spread across two meetings. In hindsight a record of some sort was waiting to be broken. It nearly didn't happen on that autumn day, for his agent had originally planned him to ride at Salisbury. Hughes didn't think his potential mounts there had great chances and asked him to see if he could find more some more likely winners at Windsor. He managed to get the ride on one of Sir Alex Ferguson's in the first race and then collected bookings for six more fancied horses.

The first two, both favourites and trained by his father-in-law Richard Hannon, went in. Then the least fancied of his rides, Embankment, scored at 7/1 in the third race, in the colours of Prince Khaled Abdulla, who used to retain Hughes as his jockey. On the 4/1 favourite in the fourth, which looked a wide open race, he powered clear to win by five lengths. That made it four out of four and he had three favourites yet to ride. It may not have been a big crowd, but excitement grew on course and among punters watching on At The Races and those following developments online. Settlers in betting shops grew uneasy as Hughes-based trebles, yankees and accumulators had to be calculated and paid out. Bookmakers cut the odds on his remaining rides.

Hughes won the fifth race. His friend Ryan Moore gave up his ride in the eighth race, possibly suffering from the effects of flying in from Canada overnight. Previously Hughes had no ride booked in it, and it was another favourite, so this meant he had a chance of riding eight out of eight, beating Frankie Dettori's Magnificent Seven at Ascot in 1996. Pat Eddery has also ridden seven winners in a day, but that consisted of three at Newmarket in the afternoon and four at Newcastle in the evening.

In the sixth race Hughes's mount Ever Fortune was beaten some way, and could only finish third. A slight sense of anticlimax descended. Riding five winners at one meeting was very rare, but it happens every ten or twenty years and wasn't generally newsworthy outside the racing media. However, the press had realised that after four or five winners, ridden by the champion jockey of all people, and with more fancied rides to come, they'd better get some photographers down to Windsor quickly.

Hughes soon dispelled any disappointment brought about by the defeat of Ever Fortune by riding the next two winners, finishing with a Dettori-style flying dismount to equal the Italian's record of seven at one meeting. (Hughes also won the first two races at Leicester the next day and added a third later in the afternoon to make it ten wins in twelve races.) The photographers and the press got what they wanted. Fortunately for the bookmakers it was a quiet Monday and betting turnover was a fraction of what there is on a Saturday, which is when Dettori rode his seven winners and cost them an alleged £40 million. Most of Hughes's rides were favourites and the accumulator paid 10,168/1. One Ladbrokes punter won £250,000 for £256 worth of combination bets. These are the horses he or she and Hughes will never forget.

2.00: Pivotal Moment 13-8jf 1st
2.30: East Texas Red 5-2f 1st
3.05: Embankment 7-1 1st
3.35: Magic Secret 4-1f 1st
4.10: Links Drive Lady 5-2f 1st
4.40: Ever Fortune 2-1f 3rd
5.10: Duke of Clarence 7-4 f 1st
5.40: Mama Quilla 15-8f 1st

Hughes had a race named after him at Windsor's final meeting of 2012 and the weighing room now carries a plaque commemorating his achievement. In 2013 he rode four winners at Windsor's 10 May meeting and five on 11 August. He finished his riding career in 2015 with 232 winners at Windsor from 1,278 rides, an 18% strike rate.

2012 was also the year in which Windsor racecourse most recently changed hands, when it was acquired by Simon and David Reuben.

The Reubens, whose family came to England from India in the 1950s, are self-made men who graduated from working in carpets and scrap metal to property before trading in metals on the stock market with enormous success. "Publicity-shy" is the phrase invariably associated with the brothers, and their few appearances in the press are usually in connection with charitable activities benefiting from the Reuben Foundation, which they initially endowed with $100 million.

The Reuben Brothers now have a wide range of international investments, but property had always been one of their main interests and in the 2000s they had started to see potential in racecourses. Property prices inexorably rise over time and tracks often have lacked investment over the years, which created opportunities for investment and thereby enhancing property values. Furthermore, changes to the finances of racing, with growing emphasis on media rights, mean that racecourses can generate good profits.

By 2007 it was understood that the Reubens had effective control of 14% of Arena Leisure but, thwarted in their attempts to acquire more, they looked elsewhere. Following the death of Sir Stanley Clarke three years earlier, whose Northern Racing company acquired several racecourses around the turn of the century, it was only natural that other organisations should be interested in acquiring them. The Reuben Brothers were successful in doing so and took over Northern Racing in April of that year.

Trevor Hemmings was the principal shareholder of Arena and, like Clarke and the Reubens, is another man to have built up a huge business empire from humble origins. His interest in racing is so strong that he has owned over a hundred horses, nearly all jumpers, including three winners of the Grand National.

The Reubens, undaunted, continued to buy Arena shares whenever they could and by 2012 they had enough to be able to buy the company with Hemmings's support. They then merged it with Northern Racing to form the Arena Racing Company (Arc). This put Arena ahead of the Jockey Club as the largest racecourse-owning group, and this year they will have 16 tracks hosting almost 40% of all British race meetings.

In February 2014 Stuart Dorn took over as Executive Director of the racecourse, having performed a variety of management roles at Fontwell and Brighton. The best horse to appear at Windsor in recent times was Al Kazeem, winner of that year's Winter Hill. Altogether he won 10 of his 23 races, four of them Group 1s (the very highest level), and most famously the Eclipse Stakes at Sandown. He was remarkable for running just as well after a year off for injury, and after another gap for a short and unsuccessful stud career.

Another of Windsor's unique qualities is that it is the only racecourse to have a gentlemen's tailor based on its premises. In 2014 the John Goodwin business, which was founded in 1947, moved into rooms with a balcony overlooking the finish. On the first floor of the Club Stand, not just on race days, you'll find Dan and Alex keen to equip customers with high quality made to measure and ready to wear garments.

For the 20 April 2015 evening meeting the racecourse threw its doors open to one and all. With the weather playing ball, almost 10,000 people took advantage of free entry, many of them sure to be first-time racegoers. This helped Windsor to record a 16% increase in its overall attendance that year, a rise that only three out of 58 other courses could surpass. The free evening was repeated in 2016.

The racecourse management wants to be actively involved with the local community and decided to support the Berkshire College of Agriculture, which as well as being located nearby is a leading equine training college. A year-long association culminated with a BCA race day in October organised by the students, with guidance from the racecourse staff.

The War Horse and War of the Worlds fireworks displays in November 2014 and 2015 have been two of the highest-profile events to help the course add value to its core business. At the time of writing a potential hotel development within the environs of the racecourse estate has been planned to leave the Castle views intact, thus avoiding the likelihood of objections. The design is also mindful of the flood plain.

In his recollections about racing Talking Horses Jeffrey Bernard describes the end of a Windsor evening meeting when he was drunk, broke, and with no means of getting back to London. Almost the last to leave, he was standing forlornly in the car park when he saw a white Rolls Royce about to glide past. He flagged down the driver, explained his situation, winding up with, "Will you please take me to the Dorchester immediately and buy me a drink." The driver took him to London, stood him a large drink at the American Bar and gave him the taxi fare home to Soho. He had never met the man before, nor did he see him again. "That is typical of what happens at the races," Bernard wrote. "It's a fairly well-known fact that racing doesn't attract many grey people … When you're on form and don't mind losing a few notes, a day at the races is one of the most magical days you can imagine."

He isn't the ideal role model, but we get the drift. Win or lose, the magic of a fine evening at Royal Windsor racecourse is one to savour.

ACKNOWLEDGEMENTS

I am very grateful for Stuart Dorn, the Executive Director at Windsor racecourse, for agreeing to commission this book for the course's 150th anniversary celebrations. Thanks are also due to Majella Baldecchino, Naomi Joyce, Mark Delin, Ronnie the head porter, Roy Clark, Shane the groundsman and the many race day gatemen and women who helped me.

I am particularly indebted to John Saville for being able to rely so much on his definitive study of wartime racing Insane and Unseemly and for the additional insights he gave me, and to Tim Cox for access to his wonderful library and for providing copies of a number of images.

The input of various members of the Knight and Stecl families was invaluable and my thanks go to Michael Griffith, Winifred Steel, Bill Freeman, Sally Maclean, Russell Knight, Sue Tyley and Karen Hoyle, with thanks to Pippa Andrews of Strutt and Parker in Pangbourne for her initiative.

Neil Pollard, Paul Davies of Thecompleterecord and Milton Johns also deserve special thanks for the time and trouble they have taken to assist me. I am also grateful to Hugo Bevan, Mick Coe, Eric Graham, Phil Grimstone, Lee McKenzie, Alan Palmer, Kirkland Tellwright, Tony Trigg, Bill Whittle, Don at French Brothers, Barbara Story and others at Windsor Library, Pam Clark at the Royal Archives, the compilers of Jockeypedia, the staff at the Berkshire Records Office and the Slough and Windsor railway stations. Online, as well as archive newspapers at the British Library and on the British Newspaper Archive, the Royal Windsor Forum have been great sources of historical information about the town, and my thanks to the latter's creator Thamesweb and its contributors such as "Nifty" for their assistance.

Thanks also to Jane Speed at PA Images, Karen Lawson at the Royal Collection Trust, David Scripps at Mirrorpix, Shakeir Ahmed at

Getty Images and the printing staff at Weatherbys. While all reasonable efforts have been made to identify the copyright holder of each image, it has not always been possible. Any omissions will be rectified in future editions.

APPENDIX 1
THE FAIRLAWNE CHASE

Year	Winner	SP	Trainer	Jockey
1962 *	Hedgelands	4/1	Cyril Mitchell	Josh Gifford
1963 *	Certain Justice	4/1	Albert Neaves	Terry Baldwin
1964 *	Sir Daniel	11/10f	Peter Cazalet	Bill Rees
1965 *	Anglo	8/11f	Fred Winter	Tim Norman
1966 *	Abandoned - waterlogged			
1967 *	Abandoned - foot and mouth			
1968	Bassnet	6/1	Alec Kilpatrick	David Nicholson
1968 *	Chilley Bridge	13/8f	Jack Cann	Buck Jones
1969	The Laird	4/5f	Bob Turnell	Jeff King
1970	Specify	100/8	Derek Weeden	Terry Biddlecombe
1971	Into View	4/9f	Fred Winter	Paul Kelleway
1972	Cardinal Error	8/1	Fred Winter	John Francome
1973	Spanish Steps	7/4	Edward Courage	Bob Davies
1974	Game Spirit	1/3f	Fulke Walwyn	Terry Biddlecombe
1975	Bula	8/13f	Fred Winter	John Francome
1976	Bula	no SPs	Fred Winter	John Francome
1977	Abandoned - waterlogged			
1978	Abandoned - frost			
1979	Joint Venture	33/1	Jim Old	John Francome
1980	Border Incident	4/11f	Richard Head	John Francome
1981	Abandoned - frost			
1982	Venture To Cognac	11/10	Fred Winter	Mr Oliver Sherwood
1983	Abandoned - frost			
1984	Everett	4/9f	Fulke Walwyn	Stuart Shilston
1985	Abandoned - snow and frost			
1986	Abandoned - snow and frost			
1987	Western Sunset	5/4	Tim Forster	Hywel Davies

1988	Rhyme'n'Reason	15/8	David Elsworth	Brendan Powell
1989	Bartres	1f	David Murray Smith	Graham Bradley
1990	Abandoned - flooding			
1991	Espy	10/11f	Charlie Brooks	Peter Scudamore
1992	Toby Tobias	1/2f	Mrs Jenny Pitman	Mark Pitman
1993	Zeta's Lad	7/4jf	John Upson	John Kavanagh
1994	Black Humour	2/1	Charlie Brooks	Graham Bradley
1995	Zeta's Lad	2/1	Charlie Brooks	Graham Bradley
1996	Commercial Artist	5/1	Nick Gaselee	Andrew Thornton
1997	Equity Player	4/1	Roger Curtis	Derrick Morris

* = the lower-value Fairlawne Handicap Chase

APPENDIX 2
THE NEWYEAR'S DAY HURDLE

Year	Winner	SP	Trainer	Jockey
1960 *	Farmer's Boy	20/1	Willie Stephenson	Michael Scudamore
1975	Flash Imp	6/4	Ron Smyth	Paul Beasant
1976	Comedy Of Errors	10/11f	Fred Rimell	Ken White
1977	Strombolus	12/1	Peter Bailey	Barry, R
1978	Beacon Light	4/5f	Bob Turnell	Andy Turnell
1979	Abandoned - snow and frost			
1980	Abandoned - frost			
1981	Celtic Ryde	4/9f	Frank Cundell	Hywel Davies
1982	Celtic Ryde	1/5f	Peter Cundell	Hywel Davies
1983	Sula Bula	10/11f	Peter Easterby	Mr Tim Easterby
1984	Secret Ballot	14/1	Andy Turnell	Ted Waite
1985	Ra Nova	11/8f	Mrs Nan Kennedy	Richard Dunwoody
1986	Southernair	9/2	Peter Haynes	Alan Webb
1987	Ra Nova	9/2	Ian Matthews	Mark Perrett
1988	Celtic Shot	5/2f	Fred Winter	Peter Scudamore
1989	Wishlon	9/2	Ron Smyth	Ian Shoemark
1990	Aldino	3/1	Oliver Sherwood	Jamie Osborne
1991	Royal Derbi	9/2	Neville Callaghan	Declan Murphy
1992	Shu Fly	4/1	Mrs Sally Oliver	Alan Jones
1993 *	Muse	1f	David Elsworth	Tony Procter
1994 *	Absalom's Lady	5/2f	David Elsworth	Paul Holley
1995 *	Abandoned - waterlogged			
1996 *	Abandoned - frost			
1997 *	Abandoned - frost			
1998 *	Halona	11/4f	Charlie Morlock	Dean Gallagher

* = run as a handicap

APPENDIX 3
THE WINTER HILL STAKES

Year	Winner	SP	Trainer	Jockey
1965	Mabel	1/5f	Peter Walwyn	Jimmy Lindley
1966	Polmak	1/10f	Harry Thomson Jones	Lester Piggott
1967	Drevno	11/2	Freddie Maxwell	Greville Starkey
1968	Chasmarella	8/13f	Tommy Gosling	Lester Piggott
1969	Midnight Marauder	3/10f	Jeremy Tree	Jimmy Lindley
1970	Merioneth	100/9	Bruce Hobbs	John Gorton
1971	Knockroe	1f	Peter Nelson	Lester Piggott
1972	Parnell	4/11f	Bernard van Cutsem	Willie Carson
1973	Sol'Argent	4/11f	Tommy Gosling	Paul Cook
1974	Punch Up	14/1	David Morley	Tony Murray
1975	Orange Bay	4/11f	Peter Walwyn	Pat Eddery
1976	Amboise	1/4f	Henry Cecil	Alan Bond
1977	Fool's Mate	4/5f	Henry Cecil	Joe Mercer
1978	Malecite	1/2f	Henry Cecil	Joe Mercer
1979	Crested Grebe	4/9f	Bruce Hobbs	Eddie Hide
1980	Masked Marvel	2/11f	Henry Cecil	Joe Mercer
1981	Royal Fountain	2/9f	Peter Walwyn	Joe Mercer
1982	Brady	4/6f	Mick Ryan	Philip Robinson
1983	Millfontaine	4/9f	Guy Harwood	Greville Starkey
1984	Alleging	5/4jf	Henry Cecil	Lester Piggott
1985	Regal Diplomat	9/4	Alec Stewart	Pat Eddery
1986	Samarid(dead heat)	7/1	Michael Stoute	Walter Swinburn
	Esdale(dead heat)	13/8f	Jeremy Tree	Pat Eddery
1987	Media Starguest	7/1	Luca Cumani	Ray Cochrane
1988	Hibernian Gold	4/1	Guy Harwood	Greville Starkey
1989	Dolpour	9/1	Michael Stoute	Walter Swinburn
1990	Song of Sixpence	11/4	Ian Balding	Steve Cauthen

1991	Filia Ardross	7/1	Alec Stewart	Richard Hills
1992	Shuailaan	2/1	Alec Stewart	Michael Roberts
1993	Usaidit	7/1	Terry Mills	John Reid
1994	Young Buster	10/3f	Geoff Wragg	Paul Eddery
1995	Desert Shot	12/1	Michael Stoute	Walter Swinburn
1996	Annus Mirabilis	85/40	Saeed bin Suroor	Frankie Dettori
1997	Annus Mirabilis	11/8f	Saeed bin Suroor	Frankie Dettori
1998	Annus Mirabilis	5/4f	Saeed bin Suroor	Daragh O'Donohoe
1999	Zindabad	7/4f	Ben Hanbury	Kieren Fallon
2000	Adilabad	6/4f	Sir Michael Stoute	Pat Eddery
2001	Adilabad	9/2	Sir Michael Stoute	Kieren Fallon
2002	Naheef	6/4f	Saeed bin Suroor	Frankie Dettori
2003	Leporello	5/2	Peter Harris	Richard Quinn
2004	Ancient World	5/1	Saeed bin Suroor	Kerrin McEvoy
2005	Eccentric	7/1	Andrew Reid	Darryll Holland
2006	Tam Lin	5/2f	Sir Michael Stoute	Ryan Moore
2007	Queen's Best	8/1	Sir Michael Stoute	Ryan Moore
2008	Stotsfold	5/1	Walter Swinburn	Adam Kirby
2009	Campanologist	11/10f	Saeed bin Suroor	Frankie Dettori
2010	Distant Memories	6/1	Tom Tate	Jamie Spencer
2011	Prince Siegfried	14/1	Saeed bin Suroor	Ted Durcan
2012	Lay Time	4/1	Andrew Balding	Jimmy Fortune
2013	Planteur	1/2f	Marco Botti	Frankie Dettori
2014	Al Kazeem	8/11f	Roger Charlton	George Baker
2015	Racing History	9/2	Saeed bin Suroor	William Buick

APPENDIX 4
FILMS AND TV SHOWS MADE AT THE RACECOURSE

1915 newsreel at the British Film Institute – available for inspection on payment of a fee

The Game of Life (1920 film)

The Fantastic Futurist (1924 film) – free to view on the BFI website.

Kissing Cup's Race (1931 film)

Pathé newsreel of a 1944 race meeting – free to view on the Pathé website.

Young Winston (1971 film)

Poirot (1993, TV) – The Jewel Robbery at the Grand Metropolitan (standing in for Brighton racecourse).

Shanghai Surprise (1986 film) with Madonna

Royal Champion (1987 TV documentary)

Last Orders (2001 film)

Midsomer Murders (2005, TV) – Season 8 episode "Bantling Boy", which included a punch-up in the winner's enclosure)

East Enders (2005, TV) with a guest appearance by bookmaker Barry Dennis

Scoop (2005 film) – Woody Allen directed Scarlet Johansson and Hugh Jackman

Celebrity Wife Swap (2006, TV) – John McCririck and Edwina Currie started their period of togetherness at Windsor racecourse

Put Your Money Where Your Mouth Is (2009 TV game show)

Outside Bet (2011 film) – set in 1985, concerns a group of friends who blow their redundancy money on a racehorse

Suffragette (2015 film) – scenes were filmed in April 2014, with Windsor standing in for the 1913 Epsom Derby

Strictly Come Dancing (October 2015, TV)

This list does not claim to be exhaustive.

INDEX